Church on the Move

Church on the Move

Leadership for Mission

JOHN FINNEY

daybreak
London

First published in 1992 by
Daybreak
Darton, Longman and Todd Ltd
89 Lillie Road, London SW6 1UD

© 1992 John Finney

ISBN 0–232–51889–0

A catalogue record for this book is available
from the British Library

Unless otherwise stated quotations from the Bible
are mostly taken from the Revised English Bible
© 1989 Oxford and Cambridge University Presses

Phototypeset by Intype, London
Printed and bound in Great Britain at
the University Press, Cambridge

To the Decade
and
all who foster sensible evangelism

Contents

Introduction
The purpose of the book ix

1 Leadership in the Decade
The Decade of Evangelism and the demand for
leadership – which requires determination, the developing
of a vision and training. The culture of the Church.
The Church as a voluntary society 1

2 Look at all the People
The nature of evangelism. What motives do people have in
seeking God? The nature of culture – its impact on the
individual. What do people believe? 25

3 Joining the Kingdom
Becoming a Christian – a theological model for practical
use 51

4 Strategy for Evangelism – I
Devising a 'Strategy for Evangelism': defining evangelism
and answering the preliminary questions 62

5 Strategy for Evangelism – II
Devising a 'Strategy for Evangelism': the six practical
questions which need to be answered 77

6 Leading for Mission
The nature of power in leadership. The French and Raven
model and the character of spiritual power. Its abuses and
uses in ministry 96

7 Managing for Mission
The characteristics of church life. The importance of middle
management and the use of line and knowledge managers 110

8   Clearing the Undergrowth
       The work of Christian leaders – its amount . . . quality . . .
       effectiveness. Using time properly. Administration.
       The dangers of workaholism   12

9   Moving into Mission
       Change means making decisions. These demand
       accountability and development training   13

10   The Spirituality of Evangelism
       The appropriate spirituality for evangelism. The acceptance
       of the pain of evangelism – and its joy   15

       Epilogue   16

       Notes   17

       Bibliography   18

Introduction

In 1988 the future Archbishop of Canterbury kindly wrote the foreword to my last book, *Understanding Leadership*. He said, 'I believe that a major challenge facing the Christian church in Britain today is that we must raise up a new breed of leaders – clergy and lay, men and women – who can harness the latent skills of local church life'. This book seeks to further this work of 'breeding leaders' so that the church is guided by people who are skilled in prayer and worship, who understand what leadership involves and have the courage to practise it. In particular it seeks to cover much more thoroughly the art of leading a church in mission.

In *Understanding Leadership* I introduced the idea of the 'flower-pot church'. It looked like this:

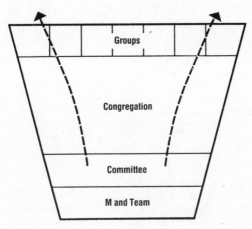

It saw the local church as an organism which was essentially moving upwards and outwards rather than hierarchical and organisationally self-centred. It saw the work of the leaders as being to support the mission of the congregation in the community. It saw the organisations of the church, including house groups, choirs, etc. as mission agencies which encouraged and trained people in their mission rather than only gave personal support to their members.

This book looks more closely at such a 'flowerpot church', and the demands which it makes upon its leaders. It seeks to be realistic, knowing that mission can be defeated as much by poor administration or negligible prayer as a lack of knowledge of the skills of evangelism.

In particular this book like the last concentrates upon people. *Understanding Leadership* thought about the members of the congregation. This book looks at least as much at those who do not come to church. It is in understanding them and seeing what God is already doing among them that we shall be able to bring God in Christ to them.

The reason is not hard to find. Even more basic than Matthew 28, 'Go into all the world and make disciples . . .', is the commandment of Mark 12, 'Love your neighbour as yourself'. If we truly love our neighbour – and our enemy – we will want to share Christ with them.

1

Leadership in the Decade

The Decade of Evangelism demands a triple miracle.

The first miracle took place when the leaders of all the churches agreed that the 1990s were to be ten years when the priority would be evangelising the world. The Anglican Bishops, the Pope and the leaders of virtually all the other churches agreed that this would be the main aim of their denominations during the Decade. It is worth noticing that this was not an initiative taken by the World Council of Churches or some such body to which the leaders were asked to give their blessing. Rather each church agreed to do this independently, feeling that it was God's will for them. If others wanted to do it too, that was fine.

The second miracle was that the Church leaders did something about it. From the time of the Synod of Jerusalem in Acts 15 there has been a tendency for Church leaders to make solemn declarations, urge far-reaching changes and then do nothing about it when they got home. In fact in many parts of the world the Church has been mobilising for mission. The Anglican bishops in the UK gathered for two days in June 1991 to discuss evangelism and the part they could personally play. From all parts of the country there have been reports of evangelism being talked about, thought about and urged upon the local churches.

The third miracle will be completed only when each local church realises what their leaders have been urging upon them and does something about it. That will take more than a few months or a few years.

I have talked of a miracle because I do believe that the Decade is of God. It has about it the touch of the Holy Spirit. Like many other initiatives of the Spirit it is easy to mock, but less easy to gainsay what is happening as churches turn outwards towards the world.

Key to the whole process are the leaders of the local churches and it is to them that this book is offered. Some are ordained, a greater number are lay. Some are paid, most are not. Some are men, some are women. But if they are not equipped to lead a church in mission then the Decade will be stillborn producing nothing.

A simple game illustrates what the Decade of Evangelism is all about. Ask a group of people to stand in a circle holding hands. Invariably they will hold hands facing inwards. Now ask them, 'Can you form the circle again but in a different way – and then join your hands again?' Every group thinks for a moment and then re-forms the circle – but this time facing outwards.

The Decade of Evangelism has at its root the desire to fix the eyes of the church on the world outside the church. For too long it has been preoccupied with its own affairs, playing ecclesiastical games which do not benefit the world. The advantage of having ten years for the Decade to achieve its aims is that it gives space for this process to begin to happen – for, needless to say, the church is not to return to being introspectively self-satisfied the moment that the third millenium has begun. Further, the ten year span means that it is far too long a time to be crammed with missions and 'events' – if that is what we think that evangelism is really all about.

Change

The Decade is about change. No doubt there will be organisational and other changes but the most important one is a change of attitude. And change threatens.

If there is no change the managing director can visit the golf club more than his office. The same goods are prepared for the same market in the same old way. Leadership becomes little more than efficiency audits and deployment of personnel. But when markets are changing, finance is tight and personnel show they are more than robots, fast-footed leadership is needed. Often changes are sudden, unpredictable and require fast decisions and immediate action. Few analysts were able to predict the changes in the Soviet Disunion and Eastern Europe even a year beforehand. It has required a total reassessment by economists, the armed forces, politicians, and even historians for we may have seen the death of secular ideologies – how few now bother about the 'isms' which ruled our thinking such a short time ago.

The Church has changed. Even the Church of England which is supposed to be so slow to adapt has changed out of recognition since I was ordained in the late 1950s. Like most traditional organisations it has done this by changing the internals while keeping the externals much as they have always been. Only when this could not be hidden, as in the liturgical changes which have taken place, has this been apparent. But the whole process of decision making, the relation between clergy and laity, the attitude towards the diocese and the bishop have all undergone radical change. Further, although this is impossible to prove, I suspect that the style of preaching, the counsel given by clergy, the 'feel' of nearly every church have also changed in subtle but far-reaching ways. It is like a beautiful building the main structure of which is retained lovingly, but which internally is being redesigned, reordered and renewed. Other churches have undergone as startling a transformation – each in their own way. The Roman Catholic Church is very different indeed from pre-Vatican II days, however traditional the present Pope seems to be. Some churches have not even tried to keep the old patterns and have launched out on new ways – the rise of the New Churches.[1]

And such change demands leadership. In the Bible little is

heard of the forty years in the wilderness. It is only when the people of God were on the march that the leadership of Moses was called upon. No doubt the intervening years required routine leadership, but it did not demand the risky decisions and 'personnel management' of the periods of movement like the Exodus or the entry into the Promised Land. Those firms which can change and evolve stay in the market-place. The main corporate virtue is not stability but adaptability. Professor Charles Handy shows that successful companies have 'core' managers who have the technical, managerial and human skills to develop new structures.[2] While it is true that some companies have been reorganised so often that there is a sense of uncertainty which means that employees cannot do effective work, and some have failed to adapt and have ended up in receivership, the successful think and work their way through the change and end up far more effective and efficient. Churches are little different. Change is inevitable because the 'market place' is altering with a rapidity which gives a premium to those who are prepared to be flexible and adaptable. But the parallel should not be overdrawn. Churches are in the main voluntary groupings and they operate by different rules than businesses where people can be hired and fired, and we shall look at the differences later in this chapter.

Dr Eddie Gibbs[3] gives a more depressing picture of the Church and puts it all down to a failure to understand the process of change and to allow for the tensions which it brings.

The church in Western Europe is changing – it is declining, aging and fragmenting. Yet this is despite an enormous expenditure of energy – nationwide missions, increasing political and social involvement, growing manifestations of the presence and power of the Spirit of God. We are misusing the energy available to us and as a result we are destroying ourselves – personally, as those who seek to apply their energies burn themselves out, and corporately, as congregations tear themselves apart in the name of progress and change, or regression and tradition. The wise use of energy requires an understanding of the transformation process.

I feel that he may be too sweeping in both describing what the Church is achieving and in oversimplifying the reason for its decline which has to do with bringing an age-old institution to bear upon society. Western civilisation is something totally new. It is secularised and yet curiously religious, culturally diverse and yet looking for a faith which unifies each culture, yearning for a law yet contemptuous of those which set standards which it feels are irksome. It is no easy task to speak to a community which does not understand itself.

Some changes are slow and evolutionary and can be accommodated. The Authorised Version of the Bible was published in 1611. It was not until the 1880s that it was realised that the alteration of the English language over the centuries had left the Church with a Bible which was increasingly difficult for people to read and more modern versions began to come available. These gradual changes are more difficult to detect. It is said that if a frog is put in a jar of water which is heated very, very slowly it will take no evasive action until it is too late. The Church is in danger of becoming like the frog – failing to perceive the decline of 'Christendom' and the need for a different strategy until it is too late.

Change not only requires leadership – it demands different leadership at different times. A disaster like an air crash demands up front, military style leadership at the site of the crash as the rescue services are co-ordinated and deployed. But soon it requires diplomatic skills in handling the media and pastoral skills in helping the bereaved and the distressed. A church moving through a period of change demands first that there is the necessary skill in coming to the right decision and carrying people with you, then the pastoral care of those for whom the change is threatening, then managerial skill in effecting the alterations, and communication skill in keeping people in touch while this is taking place. Few can do this single-handed and so the importance of a team of leaders becomes pressing. There are both scriptural and practical reasons for the use of corporate leadership but it is especially important during times of change. Therefore a further part of leadership is the ability to choose, weld together and use a team.

Mission means growth, and growth means change. Growth alters the culture of the church as surely as it alters a commercial concern. 'First there is a move from a personalized to an impersonalized approach; and then from a centralised to a decentralised way of achieving corporate objectives.'⁴ Sam Brown who ran the business and who was on first name terms with the twenty people on the staff and took all the decisions cannot act in the same way when the firm employs 2000. Nor can the minister of a church which grows remain so close to all the congregation and so involved with every decision. If the leader fails to grow with the church, either he or she will run themselves into the ground or the church will stop growing.

There are three requirements for leading a church through a period of change:

Determination

Moses leading the people out of Egypt, David expanding the petty state he had gained, Paul venturing into the Gentile world: all had a will to achieve allied with realism. They knew both that God had called them and what they had to do. This did not mean they had no inner fears and uncertainties. Indeed leaders who do not acknowledge these inner feelings tend to be brittle, autocratic and liable to sudden breakdown. Feelings can be suppressed for only so long before they emerge uncontrollably and catastrophically. Leaders of the Lord's people must know themselves. It is not, therefore, wrong to feel fearful. Paul recalling his first visit to Corinth says, 'I came before you in weakness, in fear and great trepidation' (1 Cor. 2:3). Indeed it is a paradox of the Christian life that the more the fear, the more the faith. It does not take much faith to row the church boat round and round the pond, but to take it out into rough seas is a different matter. Many Christian leaders know the feeling of being out of sight of land without a compass where God seems to have taken the church into new oceans of possibilities. It is exhilarating and frightening.

Developing a vision

The word 'lead' comes from a North European root word which means a path, a road or the course of a ship at sea. Leadership demands a sense of direction. Companies today prepare 'mission statements'.[5] These set out the aims of the business in a few sentences. It is often prominently displayed – as in a church I saw which had the statement embroidered on a banner put on the west wall so that people could see it as they went out of church. But producing a statement is not enough in itself. If you ask about it, 'whether you are met with embarrassment or pride depends on how much people throughout the organisation have been involved in developing the mission statement.'[6] The temptation is for the Board to produce a simple statement, introduce it to the rest of the company with a glitzy 'dry ice and laser' presentation and think that it is now company policy. It is said that Western management spend five minutes making a decision and six months fighting the resistance which it caused while the Japanese 'ringi system' means six months of consultation and discussion but only five minutes to get it implemented. I remember a church committee where an elaborate plan of action was introduced to the members using charts and an overhead projector. The committee sat bemused. They were bombarded with figures when many of them were almost innumerate and they were given much information in a way which few could absorb. After the presentation there was silence for half a minute – then they arose in wrath and expressed forcibly their opinion of the vision they had been offered. There is nothing wrong with a well-produced presentation, but it needs to come as a reminder to people of what they have decided. It must never be a substitute for consultation or the impersonal is taking a fatal precedence over the personal.[7]

Training for leadership

When *Understanding Leadership* was published in 1989 there was still a need to make a case for the proposition that leadership was a skill which could be learnt. This is no longer true. There is a torrent of books, courses and schemes, often produced by denominational authorities. It is now rare to come across those who would agree with General Wavell who said in 1941, 'No amount of study or learning will make a man a leader unless he has the natural qualities of one'. It has of course to be recognised that there are a number of people whose personality is such that they are unlikely to play a major role in leadership, but training can certainly make leaders out of many people who would otherwise never be considered for such a role, and it can make good leaders better. It is the person who says that they have no need of training who should never be a leader. As I have gone around the country in the last few years talking about leadership I find it is the best leaders who are most hungry for an opportunity to talk about and learn more about the ministry God has called them to. Indeed such willingness is part of good leadership. A concert violinist can already play well, but she knows it will need much practice to make her a star. Peter Drucker is right when he says, 'managers can improve their performance . . . through the systematic study of principles, the acquisition of organised knowledge, and the continuing analysis of performance'.[8]

However, it is not always as simple as that. Not all company directors (or clergy) are longing for training in leadership. Tutors in business management schools find that there are three reasons why top managers avoid learning. First, they believe their status is threatened if it is suggested that they might have a need to improve. Second, the 'trainers' are of lower status in the company hierarchy than the managers, and, thirdly, time forces training to the bottom of the agenda. The American industrial psychologist, David Clutterbuck, has said that one of the most important attributes of management is the maturity not to feel threatened. Many ministers have the same reactions.

Some churches grow leaders. They produce a stream of well-motivated and skilful house group leaders, ordinands, missionaries and in the community sturdy Christian teachers, business people and trades union leaders. Nearly always this is due to the style of leadership in the church.

It needs to be sufficiently relaxed to rejoice in the gifts of others rather than to feel threatened by them, and yet there has to be a constant desire to improve. The British psychologist, Tony Milne, found that a high proportion of senior executives were elder sons – presumably because their parents had the highest expectations of them. Perhaps it is for this reason that most leaders, inside and outside the Church, tend to be workaholics. The Christian leader needs to learn to relax, for in working to the edge of breakdown he or she is copying the world's way of working 'and it shall not be so among you'. Hours spent working efficiently are more important than the number of hours which are spent working.

All studies show that churches tend to produce clones of the minister. If he or she is an evangelist, the church produces evangelists, if he or she is a dominant personality then leadership will be seen in terms of aggression. Indeed one of the difficulties of the church is that because so many ministers are gifted as pastors they tend to produce more pastors at a time when the church may require a more directly evangelistic model. Even denominational selection procedures may be staffed by pastors, have the role model of a pastor in front of them and therefore tend to give preference to those who fit that pattern. Leaders therefore need to realise that others are copying them, whether they like it or not.

Leaders need to be clear-eyed and to have the spiritual discernment to see the potential in each person. If Christ needed to wait upon God all night before choosing his disciples how much more must Christian leaders see the discovery, training and use of other leaders as one of their main tasks. One area of discernment is often not noticed – the ability to tell when somebody is not suited to leadership above a certain level. A person may be fine as a leader of a young people's work, but lack the personality to be able to lead a church. Not all ugly ducklings are potential swans. The terrible Peter Principle, that 'everyone gets promoted to a level above their ability' should warn us of the dangers of excessive optimism concerning another's abilities.

Leaders need to be intelligent enough to realise the importance of thinking about their task. 'Every managerial act rests on assumptions, generalisations and hypotheses – that is to say on theory. Our assumptions are frequently implicit, sometimes quite unconscious, often conflicting, nevertheless they determine our predictions that if we do A, B will occur. Theory and practice are inseparable'. These words of McGregor[9] are true of every Christian leader who is making a decision. If, for example, a new house group is being set up, then theological principles about the nature of the Church, an understanding of group dynamics and past experience of the way in which groups work are all important. Too often however these basic understandings are unexamined and mistakes are made. In particular change demands examination of basic principles; only if they are looked at and either affirmed or altered will change be made.

Lastly leaders should never forget they are disciples – and the root meaning of that word is 'learners'. We must be sufficiently humble to realise that we need help from others. Today many denominational authorities provide some sort of 'in-service' training for their ordained ministers. Increasingly this is also being offered to the non-ordained, and sensible ministers realise that they should encourage lay leaders to have similar help. Sometimes pride in being part of a 'profession' gets in the way – Charles Handy saw this as one of the sins of the professions: 'professionals, self-styled or real, do not like to be "managed" with all that the word today implies of control, manipulation and direction'.[10] May God guard us from that sort of prickly defensiveness.

Leadership training consists of two parts. First there are the skills which need to be acquired, and secondly there is the development of a personality which can use them safely. Without the second the acquiring of skills can be a dangerous thing for it can provide power without the humility to use it wisely. I have taken many nurture group training courses involving 1000 people or more. It is not difficult to see those who have come in order to gain skills which will give them power over people. All power, especially spiritual power, is dangerous.

'Everyone has some leadership in them to a greater or lesser extent . . . leadership needs to be developed on a highly individual basis. There is a swing from teaching skills to developing the inner person.'[11] Those who seek training usually desire skills. They want to know the 'how to' of their ministry. Potential house group leaders want to learn about group dynamics, how to deal with the over talkative, how to minister 'in power' to the people in their group. They will feel that they are cheated when the need for personality development and prayer is talked about; 'this is not what we came for'. But it should not be avoided. Skills are important but they should not be taught without the corresponding learning of personal development.

To become aware of oneself as a human being – what sort of personality one has and what are its potentials and difficulties – is essential. Many have found the Myers-Briggs assessments useful, but there are others. (Paul saw a true assessment of oneself as vital to ministry: Rom. 12:3 – 'Know then thyself', said Alexander Pope.) One manager found that as a person he was a perfectionist and as a result was setting impossibly high standards for his staff who showed all the symptoms of emotional strain. 'Since then', he comments, 'by trying to achieve less, I've actually achieved more. Through increased self-awareness I've become a better leader.'

Many seek skills without being prepared to uncover the areas of personal need. Carl Rogers said that the most important requirements for counsellors are not skills but empathy, congruence, non-possessive warmth and the need to recognise feelings within oneself.

But more important still is to know oneself in relationship to the Lord. Some leaders look for a degree of guidance which is inappropriate and lacking in faith. They will not move until they have received prophecies and 'coincidences' galore. They fail to trust the Holy Spirit within them who is forming in them the mind of Christ to lead them into all truth. Often Christian leaders have what has been called a sense of 'touch' which means that they make the right decisions, perceive the pitfalls of the enemy and almost automatically are able to 'discern the will of God'. Others without this discernment flounder from one crass decision to the next, fail to lead their church anywhere except round in circles and engender nothing but distrust and dislike. This self-knowledge comes from a personal relationship with God. No one who truly confesses their sins before God can fail to be aware of some of the well-springs of their own character. But it is not just a matter of prayer, sacrament and Bible reading. Indeed those I have seen who have this gift in abundance seem not to be particularly pious – rather they have a commonsensical, no nonsense and very practical approach to God which enables them to relate the everyday to the eternal.

For this reason the way in which Christian leaders are trained is as important as what they are taught. The best training takes place when:

(a) it is seen to be directly relevant to the work which is being done. For ministers who have been academically educated this may not always be congenial. They may have a wish to escape into a world of ideas – the small pink clouds which can be fascinating to play with but which touch neither the reality of heaven nor the complexity of the real world. It can be an escape into a fairyland of academe. For this reason the scholastic methods of teaching may be inappropriate. They normally begin with the wide principles, and then discuss them. Only lastly do they find out the practical applications – often as a footnote to the delightful clash of ideas. The more action-centred model may be better – starting, for instance, with case studies and drawing out from them the principles which need to be addressed if those situations are to be adequately thought through. For example, the most effective way of initiating a discussion of infant baptism may be with the reality of parents wanting the best for the spiritual welfare of their child, rather than a batting around of texts from the New Testament. Start with actual experience rather than the principles. Otherwise there is the danger, which is well known in business circles, of those who have received training, leaving at the end of the session saying that they have had a most interesting day, but it not affecting their future action one whit.

(b) it is done collectively with a peer group. While training can be undertaken on a one-to-one basis or by reading books there is no doubt that people gain most if they are in a small group where they are forced to state their own position, modify it in the light of the comments of others and gain a wider experience by hearing about what others have done. This is best tackled in a small group of those who are facing the same problems. Hence generalised courses on, say, the management of change may be useful, but they are less helpful than getting together with others to work through an actual situation and seeing how the principles of 'change agency' apply. On the whole, therefore, it is best if ministers meet with ministers, evangelists with evangelists, etc. However there are reservations. Many churches have authority structures which are predominantly white, male and middle-aged. It is important for those structures to somehow have the insights of those who are female and coloured and young.

(c)   the training is done in an atmosphere of openness. The advantages of meeting with a peer group may be considerable but it can happen that a pattern of self-defensiveness evolves in which each is saying, 'they shall not see the poverty of my land'. Members of a training group need to be able to own and learn from their mistakes.

(d)   there is an atmosphere of prayer and worship so that the Holy Spirit can be seen as the supreme teacher. This is more than saying a prayer or singing a hymn before the session. It is allowing a Godward attitude to be present. One bishop always starts all meetings, including so called 'business meetings' with twenty minutes' Bible study. Others may share in the Eucharist together or have a time of silence or open prayer. The danger is that because it is a meeting to deal with 'practical' affairs this is seen as divorced from personal closeness with God – 'Let's get on with the real world'. But this is to deny the very gospel of the incarnation. The real reason for prayer and worship is the acknowledgement that all ministry is God's not ours. So easily it slips into being our skills, our personality. Only as we acknowledge from the bottom of our understanding that 'all authority is from God' will we be able to function as ministers.

(e)   there is a willingness to appraise oneself. Sigmund Freud was able to write, 'I have examined myself thoroughly and have come to the conclusion that I do not need to change much'. Few leaders are able to look in the mirror and be so smug. Many leaders wish to acquire skills. Few are prepared for the personal change which will enable those skills to be used safely. For example, many wish to become pastors but underneath there can lurk the unacknowledged wish for power which spiritual direction gives over another human being. After taking part in a leadership training course in which 150 clergy have been involved[12] there is no doubt that the most important and the most difficult part has been the acceptance of the integrity and holiness which is essential if the skills of leadership are to be used properly.

(f) there is a determination to resist any suggestion that being trained gives status. Indeed a well-trained person should be someone who is able to encourage and train others. The professional/lay distinction has bedevilled much of the work of the church as well as business life. Training should provide people with the ability to step back and let others do the work. To be captain of the team it is not necessary to play in every position oneself. Indeed it could be said that Michael Brierly was an excellent captain of the English Cricket team because he could weld together a team and did not threaten anyone with his skills!

(g) training instils confidence. One of the fruit of the Holy Spirit in Galatians 5:23 is *autarkeia*. Usually it is translated 'self-control' but this is a cold phrase. Better is 'ability to take responsibility for oneself'. Christian leaders often lack this ability to stand on their own feet because they look for the approbation of others, and their lives and decisions are governed by what they think are the expectations of others. 'The desire to be liked and the hidden fear of doing things that make you disliked is one of the major barriers to leadership'.[13]

The culture of the Church

Culture is as difficult to define as it is important to perceive. Someone described it as 'being like the back of your head – you know it is there only a few inches from your eyes but it is difficult to visualise'. Culture is the air we breathe and often we only become aware of it when we come across one that is different. I remember being acutely uncomfortable when I was beautifully entertained in an Indonesian home: the men sat down and my friend's wife and daughters flitted soundlessly behind us serving our needs. I tried to bring them into our conversation but they made no answer and it was clear that I was trying to step over a cultural divide.

Around us there is the culture of our civilisation. The work of Bishop Lesslie Newbigin has alerted us to the importance of this all-pervading atmosphere which he sees as something which can be profoundly anti-gospel. He rightly argues that the church is affected by this atmosphere far more than Christians are prepared to allow. The materialism and secularism affect the way all people think and behave – including Christians.

This whole area of Western world-view is one we shall need to look at again, but we have also to look at the more local culture of the church. In part this is denominational: an Anglican Church will have a different 'feel' to a Presbyterian one. To some extent these are the written and unwritten dos and don'ts which each church has, but it also has to do with the style of liturgy, the relationship between minister and people, the jargon which is used. In part this is social: an inner-city church will feel different from a suburban one and different again to a handful of people in a village church.

Nevertheless there are enough similarities for us to christen the Church's own culture 'ecclesiastical'. In virtually every denomination certain things are expected and others are frowned upon. Whether you are in a Roman Catholic cathedral or in a tiny New Church it is likely that smoking will be regarded as improper during worship. Certain music is permitted while heavy rock is likely to be unacceptable in Sunday worship. Interruptions to a sermon are likely to be frowned upon.

But these symptoms are only the outside of culture, the manifestations of a mind-set. For many churches the reality of

God is intellectually accepted but his action is circumscribed – indeed public worship has been described as 'keeping God at a proper distance'. The Church's general view is hierarchical – with God at the top, though too often he is seen as only an absentee landlord. Below God there is a jostling for places of authority. You are therefore unlikely to find extreme egalitarianism within the Church and in all probability there will be arguments about what men and women are allowed to do. Because of the questions surrounding authority the Church has always had difficulty in coping with innovation, and change is likely to be slow and painful.

Each local church has its own micro-climate where certain things flourish or die under the wider ecclesiastical umbrella. In one church the attitude to money is biblically down to earth and realistic, while in another there is a sense of distaste which associates it with a lack of real spirituality. In one church the leader is expected to be a chaplain to the 'establishment', while in another he or she is seen as the guru who is responsible for bringing the *ipsissima verba* of the Lord.[14]

Businesses are becoming very conscious of the importance of corporate culture. Studies have shown that in certain corporate cultures people use at best only twenty-five per cent of their potential. It is not difficult to think of certain bureaucratic systems where workers have a thoroughly busy day shuffling paper between themselves or of the laissez faire organisation which is so laid back that hours are spent in discussion and nothing is achieved. 'The culture of an organisation defines professional behaviour, motivates individuals and asserts solutions where there is ambiguity. It governs the way a company processes information, its internal relations and its values. It functions at all levels from subconscious to visible. . . . an understanding of the corporate culture is a key responsibility of leaders'.[15] It has been found that situations where there is little change produce a bureaucratic culture leading to over-control, an aversion to taking risks, and a mechanistic view of workpeople. On the other hand some companies such as 3M admire and reward innovative work, and others inculcate an almost idolatrous regard for the superiority of their products. Exxon makes its top executives take a two-week Quest workshop with the intention that they are jolted out of the 'comfort zone' into a slightly anxious frame of mind which allows risk-taking without inducing panic. Many churches find that a weekend conference or a mission audit has a similar effect.[16]

Christian leaders need to be aware of the different cultures – macro and mini – which they and their churches inhabit. Boisot has said that we can only be at home in two or three cultures.[17]

Mismatches can occur when leaders inhabit a different culture from those in their church. However hard they try they are unable to find out 'what makes them tick', and the people in the church say 'they do not understand us'. But all is not lost if this mismatch occurs. I have seen many Christian leaders who find themselves in an uncongenial situation take a full two years to come to understand and to love the new culture. But once the adjustment has been made they often come to value it more than the people to whom it is second nature. But it is not an easy transition.

The voluntary nature of the church

In *Understanding Leadership* I argued that we needed to start with a scriptural understanding of leadership before we took on board the insights of management theory. We shall be returning to management theory during this book but we need to remember that the Church is a largely voluntary body and most theory deals with a business world where there are tangible rewards and punishments for individuals and an ability to hire and fire. Like most voluntary bodies the church has a few paid employees and a large number of members who are not only unpaid, but who themselves largely provide the funds so that the objects of the organisation can be realised.

The distinctions between an industrial and a voluntary organisation are important for they highlight the nature of the church as an organisation.

Voluntary organisations exist to meet needs which are primarily social rather than commercial. Oxfam exists to relieve hunger not to make a profit. The Church exists to worship God and extend his Kingdom not to perpetuate itself as an organisation.

This basic difference has several important results which permeate the life of every voluntary organisation.

1. There can be no end to its work. Famine is unlikely to be eradicated and God's Kingdom has yet far to go before it can be said to have fully come 'on earth as it is in heaven'. Voluntary societies exist to 'do good'. Therefore their objectives are seen in terms of moral absolutes and do not readily respond to cost/benefit analysis. Indeed to fail to meet the goal only leads to a redoubling of effort. Because famine relief agencies have not eradicated hunger in the world does not mean that they stop work – it means that they work even harder. Because the church has not yet evangelised the whole world does not mean it closes down all missionary activity – it means it redoubles its efforts. Compare this with a commercial firm, which pulls out of a certain sector of the market if it finds that profit is not forthcoming. The danger clearly is that the voluntary society can waste time and money because it has no yardstick against which to measure its work.

2. Because aims can only be expressed in general terms, leaders within these organisations often have to work to ill-defined and short-term objectives. The Kingdom of God can be seen to be advanced in an evangelistic effort or the establishing of a community facility, but it is difficult to see far into the future. There is therefore a great danger that the whole becomes project-orientated. The

organisation, because its objectives are unclear, sets up short-term projects which can become ends in themselves. Churches often exist on a diet of 'events' without ever asking themselves why they are doing them. Charities are well aware of the same imperative – for the organisers it gives a feeling of well-being in having accomplished something definite. It may not do much for the blind or animal welfare but it is encouraging for the supporters to see something is happening.

3. It is therefore difficult to evaluate the worthwhileness of any piece of work. While it is true that within the Kingdom of God a mustard seed can grow into a great tree the Church has produced its fair share of great projects which turned out to be worth nothing. The attempts by some parts of the Church Growth School to set quantifiable goals have not been altogether satisfactory because the goals of the church cannot be set out in such terms.

4. A voluntary organisation tends to look for both strong leadership and yet has a built-in resistance if it comes to pass. 'It has to satisfy everyone, certainly it cannot afford to alienate anyone'.[18] The number of directors of national charities who have fallen foul of some of their supporters and been dismissed is considerable. Within the church there is a similar dynamic: strong leaders are appointed and then stopped from doing anything!

5. Because it is difficult to evaluate the work of a section within the organisation in terms of results, finances are based on budgets. For example, in a denominational structure it is unusual for, say, the education department and the social responsibility department to be assessed in such a way that greater funds are given to one at the expense of the other because it has been more 'successful'. Indeed the need to put inverted commas round 'successful' illustrates the difficulty. How can success be measured? How can one area of work be compared with another – it is like comparing oranges with apples.

Comparisons are meaningless. The financial conse-
quence is that a voluntary society typically operates
within a budget rather than being paid by results. Each
department fights for a larger slice of the cake and can,
because the needs are limitless, make a convincing case
for its own department. For a local church this has serious consequences. The amount of money allocated to,
say, the music of the church cannot be compared in
effectiveness with that allocated to the heating of the
church hall. Each demand has its own historical
apportionment in the budget of the church. Sometimes
this can be lost in the mists of time. In my own church
I discovered that a small sum had been given to an
animal charity for many years past. On investigation it
transpired that it was a charity supported by a former
churchwarden. He had died nearly twenty years before
but the allocation had never been questioned. The problem with any budgetary system is that it is very difficult
to prune one area of work which has grown over-large
because a case can always be made for its retention, and
it is very hard to build a budget for new work. After
looking at many church budgets I have found that mission is nearly always the Cinderella. Only small sums are
given to the work of the Sunday Schools, the nurture
groups or even making the church building more wel-
coming. In any period of financial stringency these are
the areas to be cut.

6. Because it is a voluntary society and people are therefore
free to come and go a church is often under the domi-
nation of a few people who use the church as a place for
driving forward their own personal or ideological
agenda. This may be a certain political or theological
standpoint, or simply a desire to make sure that their
viewpoint on everything prevails. These people cannot
be fired or shunted sideways out of the decision-making
process in the way that a commercial firm would operate.

They have to be either faced down or capitulated to. For many ministers these are some of the hardest times of their lives.

7. Voluntary organisations are particularly prone to preen themselves in their past successes. Many churches are hung about with dusty laurels – the rump of an organisation which once was full of vigour, a building which served the purposes of the past but not the present, individuals clinging to positions which once they adorned but now diminish. 'Yesterday's success becomes today's policy, virtue, conviction, if not holy writ'.[19]

I once revisited a Christian community which had been founded to serve those who visited it and be a living example of Christian harmony. When I had first gone there it had admirably fulfilled both aims. My second visit was different. The visitors were no longer there to be served: they were now tolerated only because they enabled the community to continue financially. The model of fellowship was no longer to be seen: all too visible was a body of people who had become inflexible, bureaucratic in their dealings with each other and upset by any disturbance of their normal pattern of life.

Many Christian organisations go through this pattern. Voluntary societies tend to be established for fellowship, service or campaigning.[20]

Fellowship starts because a few people feel that they have a need for mutual support and the enjoyment of each other's company. Many house groups and church organisations are started for this reason. Unfortunately it is all too easy for the pursuit of mutual enjoyment to become exclusive, their fellowship to become self-serving and their meetings to lose the freshness of the Holy Spirit.

Other groups form for service to the needs of others. Agencies for helping the mentally handicapped, the elderly and the development needs of famine stricken areas may well have a national or even international character like the Red Cross or

Christian Aid. In local churches they are often groups for dealing with a mission theme – either tackling some social problem or the evangelistic needs of the neighbourhood. These groups have to be formally organised because they have finance to raise and be disbursed. Therefore they have budgets, paid workers and a method of meeting the needs of those they are seeking to help. Sadly these organisations too can become self-serving, an end in themselves, and can absorb finance within the organisations rather than in meeting need. The ratio of administrative costs to the amount disbursed is an important figure in assessing any such organisation.

The third category are those groups which are formed for the purpose of campaigning. They try to make others aware of a need, or promote an ideology or faith, or raise money for a cause. Many missionary societies come into this category, as do political parties. As with the 'service' category these organis-ations can easily slide into raising money to keep themselves afloat, but there is another danger. Because many have a defined political or religious base there is always the question as to the 'soundness' of the message which is being purveyed. Political parties tend to examine the correctness of their mem-bers' views and exclude those which are not regarded as within the bounds of tolerance. Supporters of the Militant Tendency were thrown out of the Labour party, and 'witchhunts' and 'kangaroo courts' are a normal part of political life, especially among those holding extreme left or right wing views. Christian organisations tend to produce 'Statements of Faith' or unwrit-ten, but definite, understandings of what the aim of the organis-ation is. Since these organisations are not themselves churches they have to define themselves more narrowly than a church has to do and the person or group who is responsible for deciding whether certain people or policies are conformable to the aims of the organisation wield considerable power.

Professor Handy readily admits that each category merges into the other. For example a missionary society will campaign but also have a 'service' element in meeting the direct needs of those it seeks to evangelise. Many societies are currently debating the right balance between direct evangelism and development aid. Similarly some societies seek to emphasise the 'fellowship' which the members of the society have with each other and with those they are endeavouring to help and to learn from.

Within a local church there are the groups which develop from one emphasis to another – possibly starting as an organisation meeting together primarily for fellowship with each other, and then moving into service or campaigning. Indeed this may well be a good development for any group. However if this is taking place it is important that the members of the group are both aware of what is happening and are happy with the change. Otherwise the group is likely to split since there has been an unagreed change of agenda.

In the great passage in Proverbs 8 wisdom is personified. She is the first thing that God created and she was at his side as 'his darling and delight' as the rest of creation unfolded. In all the twists of the life of the church there is nothing that the Christian leader needs more than wisdom and her sister, the gift of discernment.

> Choose my instruction rather than silver,
> knowledge rather than pure gold;
> for wisdom is better than red coral,
> and no jewel can match her.
> I am wisdom, I bestow shrewdness
> and show the way to knowledge and discretion. (vv. 10–12)

Look at all the People

Evangelism means having 'missions'. You evangelise by inviting a well-known speaker, setting up a programme, making contacts, reaping the harvest of souls. If there is no great response it shows that the church did not try hard enough or the world is an even more wicked place than you thought. So you invite an even bigger name, set up a more extensive programme, visit more people . . .

This is caricature, but only just. This way of thinking sees evangelism as being about action not about thought. It is this activist streak which has made many of those who have a longing to share their faith shudder at the very name of evangelism. Further it has prevented many churches who have really thought about what they ought to do to reach those in their community who have no sort of faith from doing anything about it. What is worse it has given an excuse to those churches and Christian leaders who ought to be developing their own strategy, but who can point to nearby examples of hyper-energetic mission and say, 'If that is evangelism, I want no part in it'.

'The fear of the Lord is the beginning of wisdom'. Wisdom about evangelism must begin with the worship of God and his nature. In the next chapter we look in more detail at what evangelism is, but for the moment we can start with that most basic and shattering truth that 'God is love'. Therefore evangelism, like every other ministry of the Church, must show the love of God if it is to have any integrity. Love means many things, but central to them is a care for people. Just as God

loves the world and each sparrow within it so he loves all the
people of the world with a sacrificial love which we are called
to share. We are called to care for their total welfare – their
bodies, minds and spirits, but also their environment, their
situation and their culture.

This childish definition, 'Evangelism = Love', may seem
jejune, simplistic and pietistic. It certainly lacks theological
precision. But it carries within it two truths which are not
conveyed by many much more sophisticated formulations.
First, love has an element of yearning. It longs to go out to
the other in order to be with them. It is difficult to define, but
instantly recognisable. It is the voice of the bride in the Song
of Songs (8:14):

> Come into the open, my beloved,
> and show yourself like a gazelle or a young stag
> on the spice-bearing mountains.

or the psalmist longing for a closer communion with the Lord
(Ps. 42:1, 2):

> As a hind longs for the running streams,
> so I long for you, my God.
> I thirst for God, the living God;
> when shall I come to appear in his presence?

Evangelism should yearn to bring the good news of Jesus to
people. It is the same longing that Christ knew when he looked
out over the crowds and saw them 'as sheep without a shepherd'
and his whole being wanted only their good.

It is a prerequisite for a church which seeks to be involved
in mission or for the individual Christian wanting to share his
or her faith. Our more evangelical forefathers called it a 'pas-
sion for souls'. It is an old-fashioned phrase but one which well
describes the depth of this concern.

Secondly, that simple definition brings to our attention
another factor which is too often overlooked. *Those who love
think more of the person they love than of themselves.* This is

not because of any carefully worked strategy or because it has been ordered by someone else. It is the very nature of love.

In any evangelism, therefore, the person being evangelised is more important than the person doing the evangelising, and far more important than any programme or pattern. An understanding of the culture in which people live, their fears and hopes, their existing beliefs, and the barriers they may have to the Christian faith are all important. Coupled with this must be a concern for the person as a human being with all their potential and manifold relationships.

Most churches forget this. Like any human organisation they are more concerned about themselves, their growth and their impact on the community. At its worst the people 'out there' become merely a means to an end – souls to be put on the score board. They are not valued for themselves as people but as counters in an ecclesiastical game. This can apply to the evangelist totting up his 'converts' but it can also be the mindset of the minister counting his morning congregation to see if it has grown since last year, or a church committee planning a money-raising event.

It is easy to spot evangelism which does not put people first. It talks about programmes, events and efforts, and shows no sign of having first sat down and considered carefully the situation which is being evangelised. At times it has an embarrassing crassness which is doomed to failure. I once debriefed a team of people who had 'evangelised' a group of hamlets high up in the Yorkshire Dales. The methods they had used were designed to say 'look at us'. They had brought a largish tent, set it up on the village green without asking permission, brought a deafeningly loud group of instrumentalists, visited door to door without consulting the local clergy. The result was setback for the Kingdom of God in that area. Nobody was 'converted', the work of the church was hindered, and the word evangelism was branded as aggressive and insensitive. A form of evangelism which might have some validity in a street market in a city was totally out of place in a quiet village where everyone knew each other and there was a deep suspicion of 'incomers'.

Jesus told two stories. One was about the man who set out to build a tower and did not have the cash to finish it, and the second was about a king who brashly set off for war without considering that his army was smaller than that of the enemy. Some evangelism clearly has not 'first sat down and considered'. It is sub-Christian. Christ's command to love cannot be set on one side when we are engaged in evangelism. As John 3:16 reminds us, loving involves the giving of ourselves.

Further, evangelism without love is ineffective. Those being evangelised will rightly feel that they are being manipulated into joining an organisation not for their own sake but for the sake of the people in the church. They will therefore have no more desire to join than if they were being invited to become members of an ailing gardening club which is looking for new recruits.

If the people who are not in church are seen as being at least as important as those who are then they must be understood, cared for and helped as much as the insiders. That is why this chapter looks at them rather than at the church and its doings.

Positive discrimination

For centuries the church has existed for the insider. Despite the brave words of William Temple that 'the church is the only organisation which exists primarily for those who do not belong', the reality is otherwise. We play our games, get concerned and worried about matters which are of no interest to the world, run our churches for our own comfort and expect people to take us on our own terms. We are now entering a Decade of Evangelism. For ten years we need to discriminate positively in favour of the outsider. Everything the church does ought to be evaluated in the light of its impact on those who do not come. Are all our organisations looking outwards or

inwards – indeed do they need to exist at all for they absorb
Christian time and energy? Do we try to rearrange the pieces
in such a way as to make a more attractive pattern, by seeking
to provide the perfect style of leadership, or the most liturgi-
cally up-to-date correctness, or what we perceive to be the
most biblically based preaching, but forget the 'poor man at
the gate'? We may feast like Dives on the rich things of the
Kingdom but forget the millions of those who sit alongside
Lazarus.

This Decade must be a time for positive discrimination in
favour of the non-Christian. It is what the Lambeth Conference
talked about when it asked in 1988 for the Anglican Church to
move from a ministry which was 'primarily pastoral' to one
which was 'primarily evangelistic'.

Why people do what they do is central. Why do they go to
church – or become Christians – or not become Christians? It
is impossible to engage in realistic evangelism or the spiritual
care of people without being aware of the area of human
motivation.

The motivations of those seeking God

There have been many theories of motivation. One of the
most practically useful and most enduring was that set out by
Abraham Maslow in *Eupsychian Management*. It sets out the
five main areas of our lives which make us do what we do. I
have added a sixth – the need for a relationship with our
Creator, the God-shaped void which aches to be filled. Maslow
sets the five in a pyramid so that we go upwards from basic
physiological needs to the higher realms of self-fulfilment. It is
doubtful how true to reality this is. I may be seeking esteem
and respect but I still have to be fed and clothed. If I am
seriously ill, becoming healthy is much more important than
being given the deference due to my position. Our motivations

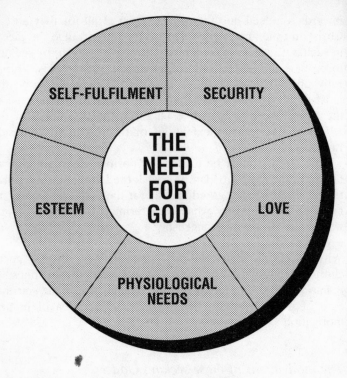

will change according to the context in which we are. Sometimes one will be uppermost, then another. Even in the course
of a single day it will change considerably. At work status may
be at the top, while in the evening I may seek self-fulfilment
at the local church and in the bosom of my family I may look
for love.

Further there is the whole area of mixed motivations. It is
unlikely that any major decision in our lives has ever been
made with only one motivation. I have often asked ministers
what caused them to go forward for ordination. They all say
that the love of God and his people was a major factor, but
none of them has ever been so brash as to claim that that
was the only motivation. Mixed motivations are normal, not

exceptional. For some the realisation of this can be a great relief for they have found themselves in the dark pit where they search for perfection. In his autobiography C. S. Lewis recounted how at school, lying in bed, he tried to say the Lord's Prayer with perfect attention to God. Time and again he tried and failed. In the end he threw the whole thing up and became an atheist.

The Bible is full of people who are more than a little mixed in the reasons they followed the will of God. Moses in the wilderness argued with God and eventually accepted his vocation, not out of sheer love for God but because God had painted him into a corner. The whole joke about the book of Jonah is that this miserable prophet had no love for either the people he was preaching to or for God. Even when his evangelism was hugely successful it made him thoroughly disgruntled. All through the Gospels there is the underlying theme from the disciples, 'What's in it for us?', and we find them disputing who was to be the greatest in the Kingdom even at the Last Supper.

These motivations are the same for the non-Christian as they are for the Christian – and so are the mixed motivations. When people become Christians it is probably not just a love of God which draws them. There are other factors at work in many cases – it may be to be accepted by their Christian friends whom they admire, the yearning for self-fufilment which sees in Christ an ideal or the church as a place of safety against a hostile world. If we are prepared to accept mixed motivations in our own lives we should not be surprised if we find the same in others.

To be aware of these motivations may aid us in our ministry to those who are coming to God and enable us to give them appropriate support and to ensure that they are able to move on from what the church as an organisation can offer to what God himself wants to give to them. It may be that the person has had an extremely insecure childhood, in which they have been subject to the break-up of their parents' marriage. They may well be looking to the church to provide the security which they lack. They want it to be steadfast, unchanging. But that is not enough. The spiritual director[1] will want to show them the God who is like a rock, 'Jesus Christ, the same yesterday, today and for ever'. Another person may come to church desperate for affection, and hoping to find in this friendly group what they have lacked all their lives. They will, hopefully, find what they seek, but it is not right to leave them there. They have to be pointed to God who is himself love. Each of the motivations are found in God as well as in the Church – he gives self-worth to those who look for esteem, healing to those who ache with physical or mental pain, direction for the lives of those who look for self-fulfilment.

It is often good practice to give the person a psalm or other biblical passage to read privately. In many instances it becomes very precious – the passage which brought them to God in Christ.

These different motivations have both a good and a bad side.

Positive	Negative
Physiological needs	
Eating, breathing, sleeping, being free of pain and with a sense of wellbeing. Spiritually it looks for healing of body, mind and spirit.	But too much sleeping leads to sloth, too much food to greed, fulfilling our physiological needs can be selfish and self-indulgent.
Love	
Acceptance into a community and the need for human warmth. Often it has sexual overtones, which are not to be seen as always negative (as can happen in Christian circles).	A craving for love can lead to a wanting to be liked, a failure to become our real self. We become the cats-paw of the wants of others.

Security

To be safe in a world full of dangers is a very basic need. The Church as an ark of safety is an ancient symbol which for many represents an essential of their faith.

Life can never be just safety. The life of faith is often one of risk, of venturing outside the safe into the unknown. It can lead to an extreme conservatism.

Esteem

The need to be looked up to and approved by others is very strong – its absence is one of the main burdens of the unemployed. We need to be valued for ourselves.

Those who find themselves only in the respect of others become the petty office holders and self-important officials of any organisation or church.

Self-fulfilment

To be able to find our real self – take responsibility for ourselves and see ourselves expand into full maturity must be one of the main needs of any adult. For many Jesus as the ideal is their goal.

The Bible talks more of self-sacrifice than self-fulfilment. To lose your life is to gain it while to gain your life is to lose it. This can be a very secular goal, however popular it may be.

Individuals may have a good or a bad image of themselves. There will be those who have a poor self-image, seeing themselves as 'bad' people. They may even identify their faults as 'sin', though it is unlikely that they will see themselves as having broken God's laws. They may be disgusted, disillusioned or dismayed by themselves without having any sense of God. They are conscious of self-condemnation rather than God-condemnation, of guilt towards the ideal person they would like to be rather than towards the holiness of God. Indeed many from a non-Christian background may well see no reason why God comes into the equation at all. It is just that they feel they have let themselves down and hurt other people and they are ashamed of it. The director will want to show them both that God can forgive them and that he can help them *to forgive themselves*. It is often the sense of the God who loves them even though they themselves do not which shows them the reality of the being of God.

There are, of course, also those who have a good image of themselves. They will cheerfully admit to minor faults and are happy to declare that 'none of us are perfect'. They appear to have very little 'sense of sin'. For the director to say that they ought to feel guilty is likely to achieve little. However, they too have a need for God, though their consciousness of needing God's forgiveness is not apparent. But God offers more than forgiveness. He offers fullness of life for the unfulfilled, love to those who feel unloved, affirmation to those who lack it. But that is of little help to those who feel life is full, basically good and who have few worries. An area of the gospel which speaks to them is the need to rejoice. The urge to worship often stems from the urge to thank someone for the goodness of life or the grandeur of a starlit night, or the beauty of a child. Harvest thanksgiving services are popular because they serve this basic human desire.

Ministers will of course occasionally come across those whose sense of guilt is crushing, and for whom the liberation of God's forgiveness is joy indeed. However for many – and probably for a growing number in a society without the Law – a personal sense of sin towards God will become increasingly rare.

The director will want to use the good areas of each motiv-ation to lead the person closer to God by showing that their need can be met in him as well as in the church of God. There is, of course, nothing wrong in the church meeting these needs – it would not be incarnational if it did not so reflect the being of God – but people need to be shown that the church is a mirror of God not an idol which is a substitute for God.

The above assumes that what people have experienced of the church has been positive. It speaks to those people who have been attracted to God through the witness of his people. This is not always so. There are those who have been hurt by the church in the past, to whom the church has been negative, unhelpful, unsympathetic or simply boring. Ministry to these people will still work with the same motivations, but they will need to find the church through God rather than God through the church. Their negative feelings will have to be bypassed for the time being and they will need to be directed straight at God. God has to be brought into the picture more quickly. There is no role model in the life of the church to point them to. Indeed, unless it is very startling, it is generally unwise to point them to examples which contradict their assumptions because they are usually ambiguous – for they will see Christians as 'only in it for what they can get out of it' etc.

The need for challenge

Part of the gospel message is a question. It can be put in many forms, but essentially it comes down to the question of the Mock Turtle in *Alice in Wonderland*, 'will you, won't you join the dance?' The picture of the Christian life as a dance which we are invited to join is excellent and accurate for it gives the sense of movement, excitement and gaiety. Long, long ago I used to run barn dances for youth groups. The music would start and after an awkward pause and much cajoling by myself one or two girls would start to gyrate. They in their turn invited others to join in and after half an hour everybody seemed to be having a good time. The Christian gospel invites the wallflowers to join in the dance of life. The Christian gospel is an invitation with an R.S.V.P. at the bottom. Baptism always has question marks, 'Do you turn to Christ?' 'Do you repent of your sins?' 'Do you renounce evil?' Christ still asks for a response as he is portrayed as doing so often in the Gospels. Somewhere along the line there has to be a 'Yes' if someone is becoming a Christian. It does not have to be expressed. For many people they move from indifference to acceptance of the faith imperceptibly, but even for them there is a need to reinforce the decision they have made unconsciously.

This baptismal challenge to conversion cannot be neglected. It is the main difference between a pastoral and an evangelistic ministry. The danger of a purely pastoral outlook is that spiritually it can leave people where they are but feeling better about it. The evangelistic ministry is helping people to move and to cope with their new experience of God.

Culture

One of the most important areas which has to be understood if we are to take people seriously is the pervading cultures within which they and we live and work and have our being.

The nature of culture

Evangelism needs to be aware of and respond to the pressures upon those who are being evangelised. It must also be self-aware, knowing that those who evangelise are not immune from the same influences. For example, in the Western world we are all subject to the effects of the Age of the Media where TV provides a common currency so that the characters of a soap opera are more real to people than their relatives, and the same news is screened from Los Angeles to St Petersburg.

More subtly the evangelists, as well as those being evangelised, are consumers, with the same pressures from the marketing departments to be acquisitive, up to date, self-centred. It is this pervasive atmosphere which leads many churches to become like supermarkets. The customer comes into the 'shop' with a list of wants. They want to pick from the shelves a little peace of mind, a sense of direction and a religious experience. If customers do not get what they want from one church then they will change their allegiance almost as thoughtlessly as patronising one supermarket rather than another. For many loyalty to a particular denomination comes far down the list and transference between denominations is common. Asking about the denominational background of people is often bewildering. If they have any such background at all they may well not be worshipping in the denomination in which they were brought up. People increasingly go to a church far more because of geographical convenience, its 'style' of worship, the character of its leadership, etc., than because of past loyalties. It is one of the ecumenical facts of life which may do much to break down the barriers of history. This seems to be particularly true in rural areas where people go to the 'parish' church – which may not be the Church of England – simply because it is local. This may represent a healthy appreciation of what mission is about – shining as lights in one's neighbourhood – rather than a lack of loyalty to one's spiritual home. A recent survey of 239 Anglicans showed that only one in five had been brought up as practising Anglicans.

Culture is not easy to describe. The classic definition runs,

> patterns, explicit and implicit, of and for behaviour acquired and transmitted by symbols, constituting the distinctive achievement of human groups, including their embodiments in artifacts; the essential core of culture consists of traditions (i.e. historically derived and selected), ideas and especially of their attached values; culture systems may, on the other hand, be considered a product of action, on the other as conditioning elements of further action.[2]

It hardly grips the attention. Yet the cultures which impinge upon us are determinative of how we behave, what values we have. Upon them hangs much of our happiness or misery. Twenty years ago I was in a church which served a vast council estate. As I baptised a baby girl I could almost say what sort of education she would have, the work she would do, the kind of person she would marry and the type of house she would live in. Furthermore I could make a fair guess at the way she would vote, her future moral attitudes and where she would do her shopping. Her overlapping cultures left her few options. They mapped out her life for her. This is less true today. Affluence enlarges choice. If you have no money there is no chance of a summer holiday; a little money opens up a few options, and increasing wealth makes possible a bewildering choice of voyages to exotic places.

Of particular importance is the tension between individual autonomy and the demands of the community. In primitive tribal groupings the individual counts for little and the survival of the tribe is all-important. There is little space for individual eccentricity and deviance. On the other hand, Western society[3] stresses the individual. There is space for people to be themselves. In many ways this is a fruit of affluence. Relative economic prosperity gives people opportunity to indulge themselves. The ideology of individualism has at the moment triumphed. The centralised economies and collective enterprises of communism have failed spectacularly and it is unlikely that socialism/communism will regain the dominant influence it had in many parts of the world.

If ideologies have really disappeared, there will be many consequences for the Christian Church. The supermarket mentality will increase as people shop around for the fulfilment of their personal needs. The church however is not a group for the selfish. It is intended to reflect the Kingdom, with its alliance between individual responsibility and corporate demands. The command to 'love one another' is its bedrock. A Christian cannot walk away from the injured world lying by the roadside. There is a stress on the need for each person to accept responsibility for their own actions and beliefs.[4]

We can see this in the cultural background of the early church. Jews had a belief in God which was rich and deep: they had a strong commitment to their religious community. To become a Christian they needed only to believe and confess that 'Jesus is Lord' – to accept him as Messiah and as the one who by his Spirit would guide and reveal the Abba. In the same way when people have been brought up within the Church, then the completion of the initiation process is inevitably going to be their own personal acceptance of their inheritance through true repentance and faith.

But the New Testament is not only a gospel to the Jews, it is a gospel to the Gentiles. The belief patterns varied widely from the sophisticated agnosticism of Athens to the superstitions of the countryside and the love of the occult seen in many of the mystery religions. Here the Christian evangelists could not count on any basic knowledge. The gospel went first to the Jews, secondly to the godfearers who were adherents of Judaism, with a belief in one God, Creator of the world. It is when the synagogues were no longer open to them that Paul and his companions turned to the wider world.[5] Two things were evident. Where 'church growth' was concerned the market place was much more receptive to the gospel than the synagogue, and churches were founded all over the Gentile world with extraordinary speed. In only a few years the Jews, who had formed the majority of the church, became a small minority, though Jerusalem remained a Christian centre, despite the catastrophe of AD 70.

The gospel did not change but the emphases of the Christian preachers did as they adapted to the different cultures they encountered. The evidence in Acts is tantalisingly limited but the sermon on the Areopagus in Acts 17 is totally different in feel and content to those which he is represented as preaching in the synagogue, or which were preached by Peter at Pentecost or Stephen before his martyrdom. He preaches a sermon which takes its text from a pagan altar and refers to his own experience in Athens. He begins with their own thought forms by emphasising the universality of God and uses, not Scripture, but a quotation from the Greek poets to confirm his argument. He speaks of the 'Day of the Lord' as a day of judgement and of the need for repentance. Only after this does he refer to

Christ as the one who has been raised from the dead. There is no apparent reference to the crucifixion or any other of the main Christian themes.[6]

The impact of culture upon the individual

A diagram will illustrate the many forces which act upon us:

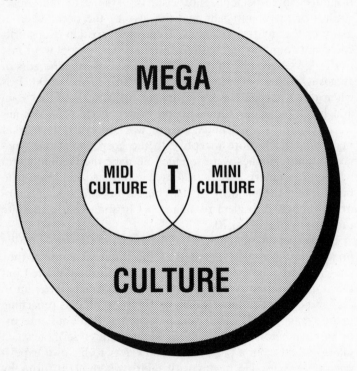

The outer circle represents the mega-culture. It can loosely be called 'Western civilisation' – the child of the Enlightenment. It shapes the way we think and behave: it sets the standards we communally accept, whether it be on the treatment of criminals, our attitude to sexuality or our desired standard of living. The midi-culture is more local. Only one is shown in the diagram but in fact we live in many, and we move freely between them. We behave differently towards people when we are shopping in a consumer orientated midi-culture than when we are in church with its own set of values and expected behaviour. The boardroom has a different midi-culture to that of the shop-floor, the pub to that of the concert hall, the football club to that of the church house group. This is not just a matter of doing what is expected of us but of different ways of thinking and relating to others. It is easily seen in the life of the church when people speak and behave towards each other differently after a service in church compared to a social or a business meeting.

The other small circle is the mini-culture of our own family grouping. Children are often surprised when they go to the home of another and find very different norms and expectations. Each of us lives in our own mini-grouping. Where this is removed by divorce or death, a child will be deeply disorientated: the usual patterns are broken and he or she is unsure of themselves – sometimes for the rest of their lives.

A director needs to be aware of the various circles which the person they are with inhabits. Often we are only aware of a small fraction of a person's life – usually their home situation and one or two of the midi-cultures they inhabit. All too often we have little idea of the midi-culture of their work situation or of their leisure time surroundings, yet these are of the greatest significance to the way they react.

This understanding of the cultures an individual lives with is a showing of the love of God for the person, but it is also sensible. D. T. Niles said, 'If you are working with a piece of wood, you must work according to the grain; otherwise you only get splinters'. Evangelism without wisdom about those being evangelised produces sharp, bitter needles which injure and goad. It can even be counter-productive in that people are pushed further from the Kingdom rather than drawn to it by the magnet of the Lord Jesus.

Above all there needs to be insight into the 'Western culture' which is at the centre of the lives of all of us.

The gospel and Western culture

That all Americans and Europeans live in a Western culture is undeniable. There are various differences across countries and within them, but the same values are the norm throughout. This norm is pounded home, and to some extent led, by the media. Lesslie Newbigin has argued that this culture is profoundly non-Christian, even anti-Christian. The current 'plausibility structure' for instance is deeply suspicious of the miraculous and in favour of pluralism. The cardinal virtue is tolerance, and anyone who suggests that there are standards and boundaries which it is illegitimate to go beyond will be regarded as a fanatic and savaged by the interviewer and the audience in a late night chat show. The treatment of Mary Whitehouse in Britain and of the pro-life campaigners in the US and elsewhere show the lengths to which this will go. It is regarded as intolerable for people not to be tolerant of everything.[7]

An understanding of this all-pervading scientific culture is essential to gain insight into the way in which people think, behave and need help. For example, if someone has the 'normal' view of tolerant behaviour they will be highly resistant to a gospel which starts by defining closely the standards of the Christian life. Therefore a sermon on total honesty and chastity will be automatically rejected as 'puritan' or 'illiberal' or 'interfering with the human rights of others'. The director would be better to start with the person of Christ – for the picture of the ideal human character lived by these standards will be far more attractive than a series of 'Thou shalt nots'. Indeed, it may be best not to refer to these standards but to stress the joy and peace of the Christian life knowing that the person probably has an image of the Christian life which is negative, life-denying and grey.

Lesslie Newbigin's books are the best introduction to the subject.[8] However, it may be necessary to sound warnings.

First it is clear that while the media and the scientific world are generally entirely at home in the deep blue sea of Enlightenment, these are not the bulk of the population. Most people have not become atheists. They may have ceased to be Christians but they do not believe in nothing, which might be assumed to be the logical thing to do. In a recent conversation the Secretary of the Humanist Association assured me that people were turning to 'things which were even worse than Christianity' – a back-handed sort of compliment. She is right. People have not turned to the cool, antiseptic universe of pure reason which the atheist looks for. Instead they have populated the world with a legion of astrological influences presided over by a god they call Fate. Belief in something beyond this material world is widespread. A survey of Scottish students showed that 95 per cent believed in the supernatural. Nor is this superstition diminishing. All evidence suggests that this is becoming increasingly common. Chesterton's famous dictum is coming true, 'When they stop believing in Christianity they don't believe in nothing, they believe in anything.'

At worst this is a flight into the irrational. But Christians should not be too quick to condemn entirely for at its best it is founded upon a very biblical sense of wonder. It is summed up for many in the Green Movement. This seems likely to persist and grow, not necessarily in terms of votes, but in terms of influence upon the thought processes of our world. It teaches that the world is both wonderful and delicate while humankind is uncaring and foolish. It is not difficult to see those very themes in the Bible, when it speaks of God creating all things 'very good' and human sin defiling the glory of it all. It is only when it goes beyond that into the metaphysical that it enters more questionable ground. There are some who call nature their God, name it Gaia, and worship it. But that is not the only reaction – there are many who find their way into the Christian faith because of the realisation that the beauty and delicacy of the created demand a Creator and the mess we have made of the planet demands a Saviour.[9]

Secondly, Western culture is not static. It is a moving target, not least because of the information revolution which has already transformed half our lives and looks set to transform the other half. It is ironic (or prophetic) that Blake saw 'eternity in a grain of sand' – and sand is mainly silicon. A distaste for science has settled over many as it appears to create for us a more and more comfortable cocoon but one which is increasingly out of touch with the reality of the earth, the sky and the sea. New 'plausibility structures' may be emerging. It may be that science is now regarded as unknowable, and the activities of the scientists as mysterious as the doings of the alchemist were to the peasant on a medieval farm. The inevitably increasing specialisation of the sciences already means that they find difficulty in speaking to each other, let alone to those without their training. Certainly there is already a move towards a more holistic view of life which does not see human beings as mere mechanisms, and which is closer to the biblical doctrine of humankind with its insistence on the unity of our being and the sense of individual responsibility and destiny.

It may also be true that Western culture is becoming less homogeneous. In part this may be because the midi-cultures have become more important. For example, there is little common language for communication between an exponent of modern youth culture, a follower of Islam and the outlook of an old soldier. Yet all three may be represented in a single street. Each becomes more distinct as though we prefer to live in cultural villages now that few can live in real villages. It gives a sense of belonging, though the counterbalancing exclusivity which is part of the mentality of the inward-looking community does not bode well for social cohesion. Paki-bashing and the vigilante groups which have grown up in response may be straws in a foul wind.

Further, for many the mini-culture of family has become the determining area of influence. The D.I.Y. generation beautifies its house, and keeps itself to itself. It identifies with no group and belongs only to itself. Socialising only takes place at work: all other contacts are within the family.

There is a footnote to this where the church is concerned. It has always tried to provide a single worship setting which would be equally acceptable to every midi-culture. Rich and poor, young and old were able to come. There were good theological reasons for this – 'all one in Christ Jesus'.[10] However unpalatable it may be, there may come a time when it is impossible to keep the different midi-cultures together in one act of worship and the ideal of 'all God's people around God's table on God's own day' may no longer be feasible. Already young people worship in a very different way to those who are older, the ill-educated in a way which is foreign to the educated. This is seen in the continuing debate about what is appropriate music in church, what part the minister should play and the style of worship which is 'right'. It is clear in some places that a form of worship which really satisfies nobody is no longer acceptable, as people leave in search of something where they can feel completely at home. This forfeiting of a precious ideal will be hard for those to whom the unity of the congregation, seen in terms of people at one service, is rightly precious. But it may be that visible unity has to give way to something which is more accessible for the different groups which we have in our population.

Belief patterns

A consideration of culture leads us on to think of the belief patterns which are within our society. What do people actually believe about God? What proportion of the population know the bare bones of the gospel?

The director will be speaking to someone who comes within the diagram on p. 46.[11] It need hardly be said that, since people's beliefs are uncertain and difficult to uncover, the

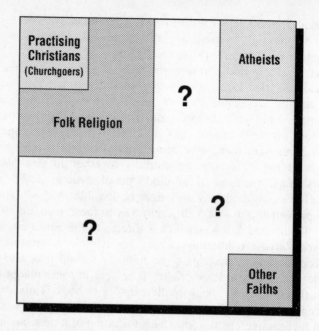

diagram must be very approximate. However, it is important to make some attempt to define or we may fail to realise what people we encounter actually believe. The square represents the whole population of England – no doubt other nations can compose one for themselves.

To start with the smaller square in the top left-hand corner, the number of regular churchgoers is about ten per cent of the population. They are likely to be aware of the fundamentals of the faith and have some experience of prayer and the presence of God. However, they should not be taken for granted. As we saw earlier in this chapter many come to church because of motivations which do not necessarily embrace a true belief in God. It is all too easy to parrot creeds or statements of faith which mean little or nothing in the life of the person concerned. The church must be a field of evangelism as well as the world. The Roman Catholic Church has understood this thoroughly and sees much of the first part of the Decade as being the evangelising of the Church. By this they do not mean just bringing people to a personal faith which corresponds to their baptism; they mean helping people to so get to grips with the gospel that they are living lights for Christ in the church and the world. Even in churches which are thoroughly evangelical it is surprising how many are encountered who have no living knowledge of God or are unaware of the need to relate their faith to their life.

The larger square in the same corner comprises those whom I have labelled 'folk religionists'. There are many definitions of this group. Some call it those who have a 'common religion' or 'implicit religion'. Facetiously I call them the people 'who feel guilty when the minister calls', for their conscience tells them they ought to be in church. They are those who have a knowledge of the Bible, probably went to Sunday School or church in their youth, may still come along to church for special occasions. They may well pray, and when they do it will be to God the Father through Christ. This group varies from one part of the country to another. Generally it is larger in the north than the south, in the country than the town, and in the suburb than the inner city or the estate. It is also markedly higher among the old than the young: in the 1950s more than fifty per cent of children had an active involvement with a Christian church – at the end of the 1980s it was down to fourteen per cent.[12] In other words young people in inner-city London are likely to have virtually no knowledge of the faith while elderly people in Cumbrian villages are likely to retain a good deal. There seems little doubt that this proportion of about a quarter of the population with a folk religion is declining. It has certainly gone down considerably over the thirty years I have been ordained.

The 'atheists' square I have set at ten per cent of the population. It is very difficult to quantify. Certainly the numbers of atheists who are active enough to join the Humanist Society or a similar body is tiny. Those who were communists thought of themselves as atheists, but they are now few indeed. There are not many who wish to inhabit this rather bloodless world. As someone brought up as an atheist I remember both the little brown books of the 'Thinker's Library' and the bleak outlook they promised. Bertrand Russell wrote one called *Why I am not a Christian* in which he said, 'the only sure foundation is unyielding despair' – at least he had the courage to follow his logic through to the end. It is more common in the academic world than outside it, and possibly more common among men than women. But a thoroughgoing atheist who gives no ground to any superstition and who believes in nothing outside this world is not that common. Many who have seen the diagram have suggested that my figure of ten per cent is in fact too high.

The 'other faiths' corner is comparatively small. About three million of our fellow-countrymen and women are, more or less, practising members of non-Christian religions. It also has to be remembered that they have their 'folk-religionists' in the same way as the Christian faith. Most faiths are reporting that people, especially the young people, are not coming to the mosque, the gurdwara and the synagogue as often as they used to. It is important for Christians to remember that the numbers in this corner are comparatively small. While the presence of other faiths is of great significance in some areas they are fairly limited geographically. There is some danger that we concentrate so much upon other faiths and the very real questions they pose to the Christian faith that we forget the much, much larger body of our fellow-countrymen and women who inhabit the remainder of the square.

It is the '?' group which is most interesting. I am sure that this group has always existed but it is vastly larger than it used to be. These people have virtually no knowledge of the Christian faith, yet many of them pray.[13] When they swear they usually blaspheme 'Christianly' using the name of Jesus or of Christian symbols like the blood of Christ but know nothing of who or what they are invoking. The level of superstitious belief is extremely high – astrological and New Age outlooks are common. Language about 'auras' and 'channelling' are borrowed from spiritualism. Any bookshop shows the popularity of books on unusual happenings with the suggestion that they have some extra-terrestrial or supranormal explanation. Industrial chaplains report that a surprising number of top industrialists will not enter into a major deal until they have consulted their clairvoyant – a practice which is not unknown even in the White House. One clairvoyant I encountered had clients coming every half hour from 8.30 a.m. to 8.30 p.m. with an hour off for lunch – and they paid for her time.

All groups (including the churchgoers) are likely to have an uncertain and contradictory set of beliefs. But this group, because it has no central philosophy, is likely to be more confused than the others. A racing driver claimed to have no belief in anything, yet refused to drive unless he had his lucky mascots. A belief in ghosts is found in the same mind as a belief in 'when you've gone, you've gone'. Into this scrambled chaos can come the Holy Spirit to bring truth out of confusion.

I have indicated that this group comprises about half the population. It is likely to be higher among the young than the old and therefore to be increasing. Whether, in fact, it is forty or sixty per cent matters little: it is a massive fraction of the population and we cannot ignore it.

The director who encounters those from within this group will need to remember that there are no resonances. A phrase like 'the cross' or 'the Good Samaritan' means nothing. It cannot be expected that the concept 'God' has any meaning whatsoever; 'sin' has no personal significance and 'life after death' is as likely to mean reincarnation as a more traditionally Christian view.

Further those within this group are likely to have no experience of the Christian church. An occasional wedding or funeral is likely to be the only time they have been in church. They do not know the expected patterns of behaviour – hats off, speak quietly, look serious. If they came to a service they would not know where to sit, nor the 'well-known' hymns, nor the difference between an old liturgy and the new. They may well not know the Lord's Prayer. A church is an alien and threatening land.

This does not, of course, mean that they are particularly resistant to the message of Christ. Indeed because they are not innoculated they may respond better than those whose view of faith has been tainted by some experience at school or through a family horror story about 'when I was made to go to church three times every Sunday'. But the evangelist or director cannot take anything for granted. To tell them to 'read their Bible' is little help to those who do not have one and cannot handle one.[14]

This group may be forty or fifty per cent of the population, and it is growing. With them the Decade will succeed or fail.

3

Joining the Kingdom

Before moving on to consider the way in which we can produce a strategy for evangelism it is helpful to look at what we mean by bringing someone into the Kingdom of God. Otherwise we shall adopt partial and insufficient models of evangelism.

For example, has somebody *really* entered the Kingdom of God if:

(a) they went forward at an evangelistic rally but did nothing about it later?
(b) they were baptised as youngsters but never went near a church thereafter?
(c) they had a great experience of God as an adult but it merely remains as a wonderful memory rather than a spur to action?

It is not enough to say 'all judgement is of God and so we do not know'. That is true but if we rely on that, we have churches full of the half-converted. It can prevent us looking at what the Bible really says, for it confirms none of our tidy theologies.

The difficulty is the New Testament. It has several different emphases not a simple 'plan of salvation' which can be universally applied. It is more human, more real, and more complex than our neat programmes.

It may be helpful to have a diagram to illustrate at least some of the themes in the New Testament. It would be foolish to expect that any diagram can be adequate to the Bible's grandeur and subtlety but it is useful for the evangelist and the director to have a model in their mind which enables them to

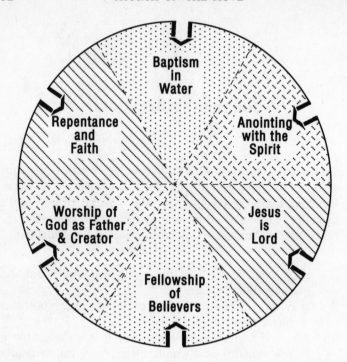

begin to see something of the direction in which they may encourage the person they are helping.[1]

Note that the segments are in pairs on opposite sides of the circle: for example, 'Baptism in Water' is linked with the 'Fellowship of Believers'. The top three are the controlling segments which lead to the lower segments: hence 'Repentance and Faith' leads to acknowledging 'Jesus as Lord', and 'Anointing with the Spirit' to 'Worship of Abba'.

Please note also that all the lines inside the circle are dotted to show that one can move from one segment to the other at will, and also that one can enter the circle from outside through any of the gateways.

There is not space to enter into a full description of each segment. That would require a book on Christian initiation –

indeed many more theologically thorough books on the subject are urgently needed. However it is not difficult to see that the 'Baptism in Water – Fellowship of Believers' axis emphasises the **corporate** nature of the faith. Such passages as Romans 6 show that baptism is much more than just an opportunity for either public profession of faith or giving a baby an insurance certificate. It is the sacramental entrance into the Body of Christ in which the catechumens die to self in the waters of baptism and rise again to new life in Christ within the body of the church. Those who are Catholics in their attitude find that this is the foundation upon which they build their faith. They point out rightly that the Bible shows that faith is lived in community not isolation, and that the sacraments of grace are the 'glue' which holds the Body of Christ together.

However most evangelicals would feel happier in the 'Repentance and Faith – Jesus is Lord' axis. This emphasises the **personal** response to the love of God in Christ. For them this confession of faith must be overt and declared. They are suspicious of the Catholic attitude which seems to them to be dangerously lacking in personal responsibility. They point with justification to the call of Christ to 'Repent and believe the gospel' and the preaching of the early church which cried 'repent'. The early creed was 'Jesus is Lord', and nothing should take away from the need for conversion in the acceptance of the free gift of God won for us on the cross. The Catholic would retort that this is all dangerously individualistic and too much depends on the human response and not enough on the free grace of God.

The 'Anointing with the Spirit – Worship of God as Father and Creator' axis is more diffuse. It concentrates on the 'baptism of the Spirit', or whatever other term is used to describe the inrush of the Holy Spirit – a direct **experience** of the being of God through his Holy Spirit which enables the individual to worship with a new freedom and to rejoice in the world and its Creator. Its central texts are Acts 2:38; 10:44ff; 11:15ff; 1 Corinthians 12:4–11. This is the Pentecostal strand of

Christianity which Lesslie Newbigin identified as long ago as
1952 in *The Household of God*. The Pentecostal/Charismatic
would say that the other two axes can be too wooden and
cerebral, and lack the free flow of the *ruach* of the living God
– the unpredictable but life-giving wind which sweeps in from
the desert.[2] In turn the others would say the Pentecostal is far
too dependent upon experiences and not sufficiently grounded
in Scripture and tradition.

The diagram suggests that all are right in what they affirm:
we do need to repent and be anointed with the Spirit and be
baptised. Indeed the baptism service has all these elements
within it. But any one of these axes taken by itself is defective.
The criticisms which are made are accurate. The Catholic can
be too mechanical, the Evangelical too individualistic, and the
Pentecostal too experiential. But together they form a strong
ground for initiation.

Frequently I have used this diagram with a group of people.
The thing which seems to give most help is that it affirms where
they are. They may have only entered one segment, but I can
say, 'That is excellent but God wants us to enter into all the
segments'. It may be that someone has entered the church
fellowship because they are lonely, or because they have a
friend in the congregation. They value the companionship and
the social events which the church holds. To such a person we
can say that we are pleased that they are part of the fellowship,
but that the other areas also need to be explored. For some
people one axis is all-important. Again we want to affirm where
they are but go on to encourage them to explore new outlooks
on the Christian life. For some this can be a revelation. An
Evangelical starts exploring Catholic spirituality, a Catholic has
a real experience of repentance and faith in which all that she
has said and believed in her head becomes true in her day-to-
day living and the Bible springs into life. Both may need to
receive the laying on of hands with prayer for the infilling of
the Holy Spirit so that they can worship and exercise the gifts

of the Spirit more readily. Ultimately we want both them and ourselves to experience and move freely in all six segments.

When I am using the diagram with a group, I first ask them to indicate the axis with which they are most comfortable. This can be a surprise to the church leadership. One church which has a name as strongly evangelical found to the consternation of its leaders that a third of its people saw the basis of their faith on the 'baptism/fellowship' axis. An Anglo-Catholic church I visited found that well over a quarter claimed to found their faith on a Pentecostal understanding of initiation.

I then ask people to indicate:

(a) those segments which they need to learn more about. People tend to tick two or three. These then form the basis for further teaching and ministry. On occasions with a large meeting I have split them into three groups corresponding with the three axes and have arranged for each of them to be led by someone who can both teach and minister. Alternatively, of course, the areas where there seem to be questions can form the basis for further teaching within the church.

(b) those segments which they need to revisit. For example, someone may have had an experience of repentance and faith long ago which has lain fallow, or a baptism which has never been carried through, or a Pentecostal experience which has not been built upon.[3] There is a real need for those people who feel they have 'got beyond the sacraments' or who see themselves as 'post-charismatic' or who have rejected their youthful commitment to God in Christ to go back to their roots. The Christian life means incorporating one's spiritual history as one grows in Christ, not repudiating it.

(c) those segments of which they are fearful. For some this may be the sense of public commitment involved in baptism, or a fear of the Pentecostal area because they feel they will be 'losing control' or of repentance and faith for they shrink from what they think God will demand of them. They need careful and sensitive teaching which enables them to overcome the barriers to visiting that segment and making it their own.

However the most important use of the diagram is in helping those who are coming into the circle of Christian initiation *for the first time*. It is interesting to see the various directions from which they come. It is also noticeable how many opportunities Christian leaders are given in their everyday ministry which can lead someone into the circle through one or other of the gateways.

Baptism in water

There will be those who ask for baptism. It may be their way of asking to become a Christian. More likely it may come from a sense that a culturally determined something is missing from their life – they were not 'done' when they were a child. Less than forty per cent of children are baptised in any church these days and the percentage is diminishing. The number of the unbaptised is growing. It should therefore be natural when ministering to ask if someone is baptised: it may well be that they do not know what the word means and the explanation will itself say something about the nature of the free grace of God in the gospel. The need for preliminary education can then lead into a nurture group or the catechumenate.

There are also an increasing number of 'family baptisms'. Often it begins with a baby being brought for baptism. Enquiries show that other members of the family are also unbaptised, and it is not uncommon for whole families to be baptised together. I can remember an occasion when three generations in a family were baptised together: it was a time of deep rejoicing.

As in the case of the other axes the next step when someone enters a segment is normally to lead them to the other half of the axis. In this instance they need to be led into the fellowship, and made to feel part of the family before moving on to explore different segments.

Repentance and faith

It has already been suggested that there are fewer people who have a deep sense of guilt towards God than was the case when Christian upbringing brought home the standards and the holiness of God. However this does occur, and even more people are aware of their own unworthiness and lack of personal integrity. Often this is either internalised – 'I do not come up to my own standards' – or directed at others – 'I know how much I have hurt X' – rather than at God but nevertheless the offer of forgiveness and personal freedom from guilt is a lifeline.

Most 'standard' evangelistic methods concentrate on this area. While they are particularly appropriate among those who have some Christian understanding others also find the Pauline cry is theirs, 'Who is there to rescue me from this state of death? . . . there is now no condemnation for those who are united with Christ Jesus' (Rom. 7:24, 8:1).

Those who enter into this segment first require particular care. They are tempted not to journey further – they feel a sense of release, they are thankful to God, but they may feel little need to move on to other areas of faith. They have their freedom – they require no more. It is important to lead such people quickly on – probably first to the acknowledgement of Jesus as Lord for they need to know the gospel is not about feeling better but about the centrality of Christ. Beyond that they should probably be introduced to the corporate area so that they make that aspect of faith their own.

Anointing with the Spirit

Most Pentecostals would regard this as a definite episode in someone's life when they experience the 'baptism of the Spirit'. Some would say that in all cases it will be accompanied by speaking in tongues. Modern Charismatics will be much less dogmatic. They will see the experience as either sudden or gradual, and speaking in tongues will not be a required desideratum. They will expect, however, something perceptible to happen and will look for the gifts of the Spirit to be manifested in some way.

The widespread nature of this phenomenon has to be accepted. The *World Christian Encyclopedia* suggests that over twenty per cent of Christians have a basically Charismatic spirituality. It is a segment which can cause unease but there is also much evidence of churches renewed and individuals transformed.[4]

There are a surprising number of people to whom this segment is the gateway into the circle. For some it is a classic Pentecostal experience while for others it is a 'religious' phenomenon which is much less easy to categorise. It may be a dream or an irruption of the spiritual which leaves them breathless. Research by the Alister Hardy Institute states that over forty per cent of the population have had some such experience, and there is some evidence to suggest that the figure is as high as sixty per cent if people are given the privacy of a confidential interview. It can be so overwhelming that they are reluctant to talk about it for fear of being thought unstable or odd. Frequently they will preface their story by saying, 'You won't think I am mad, will you, but one day . . .' or 'I have never told anybody this, but . . .' They have a sudden awareness of the spiritual. Often there is little intellectual content – 'God took me and threw me against the wall' as the novelist Susan Howatch said. Whether it is a Pentecostal event or incapable of being pigeonholed it can be life-changing. It can suddenly catapult people into the circle, in contrast to others who enter at a snail's pace.

Worship of God as Father and Creator

The need to worship is universal. Even 'the self-made man worships what he has made'. The object of this worship can be good and wholesome or rancid and foul. It is for this reason that the Fatherhood of God has to be put in front of people – the Father Almighty and All-holy, perfect in love and justice, the one who knows and cares when a sparrow or a star falls.

The concept of Fatherhood is, of course, difficult for some, though I have found that the experience of an absent or a violent father does not mean that the idea is best forgotten. Indeed for some it seems that they need the ideal Father to correct the image of the human father who has failed them. It should not therefore be avoided unless it is an obvious point of difficulty. If so they can perhaps find the Father through the work of the Holy Spirit later in their Christian walk. For many the love of the Father draws them still and it is through this gateway that they come.

The modern ecological movement has greatly heightened our awareness of the creation. At its best it has interested people in the wonder of the creation, and many are finding a thought intruding, 'Perhaps behind all this beauty which we have tarnished there is a Creator'. While the temptation is to worship the creation rather than the Creator, as Paul said in Romans 1:25, there are those who find themselves entering the circle of initiation through this door.

Jesus as Lord

As the Father can be the perfect Father, so Jesus can be the ideal human being. Since he is more 'visible' in the pages of the Gospels he can be more easily imagined and sought. Without sin, he was not icily, untouchably perfect but totally and warmly human.

Few people can look in the mirror unmoved. There we see someone who is less than he or she might have been. Those who have this sense of a lack of worth find in this aspect of the good news a way to greater self-acceptance in obedience to the Lordship of Christ. Often these people will respond to the Gospel stories of the disciples 'leaving their nets' and following Jesus or of the heroes of the Bible venturing all in obedience to God. At the root of this great confession is the need to put ourselves beneath the reign of the King of the Kingdom.

The fellowship of believers

Some are brought up in the life of the church. Others come into it later in life because it provides a social grouping which accepts them, or represents something they are looking for: a body of people who are seeking, however inadequately, to love one another.

Christians often play down the church. They are only too well aware of its deficiencies and the lack of true holiness. But those who come in from outside may have a truer picture. Again and again I meet people who were drawn to the faith by the reality and atmosphere of the fellowship. Those inside the church would repudiate any such description for they are only too well aware how far they still have to go. But the warmth of the fire of Christian fellowship still attracts.

It is easy to speak contemptuously of such people, who seem to be in the church for what they can get out of it and who seem to have journeyed along so little of the Christian path. Christ would not do so. He would both have recognised the genuine search for truth which comes through the person looking for friendship and he would have been well aware of the fact that the same needs are in us all.

Obviously there is a danger that those who enter through this gateway do not progress beyond the segment of fellowship into the wider reaches of Christian discipleship. They need to be shown that the people they admire are who they are because of their faith, and that this can be theirs as well. They can be encouraged to experiment with prayer until they see that it is an aligning of our will with God's. They can be shown that behind the routines of worship in the church there is a reality which can speak to their lives.

The fullness of Christian initiation is of the greatest importance. Evangelism is only partial if it does not bring people into all their inheritance. Further we need to learn the art of helping people through this critical stage in their lives. It requires care and courage to act as a midwife until they 'come to have the form of Christ' (Gal. 4:19).

4

Strategy for Evangelism – I

'A church exists by mission as a fire exists by burning' . . . 'A church that lives to itself will die by itself' . . . There are endless exhortations to evangelism. They generate guilt, give a sense of failure and achieve little. It is extraordinary that one of the greatest evangelists spent very little time commanding those in the churches he planted to evangelise. The Pauline epistles are full of solid Christian teaching on how to live the Christian life in the community rather than exhortations to go out and 'win the world for Christ'. Possibly we need to learn from him that evangelism is not principally the work of individual evangelists – it is a community living out its faith. A Christian church which is grappling with the problems of its members acting in love towards one another and the community will be evangelising in a natural, unforced way. I remember a meeting at which a well-known evangelist talked with the ministers of the main churches of a city about leading an evangelistic campaign. In the end he said, 'I am sorry, but you are too divided, your morale is too low, your churches are too unsure of themselves for you to undertake any effort of this kind.' Christian leaders need to learn from Paul that the first task in mission is to seek to grow a healthy church.

Each church needs a strategy for evangelism, but before it starts on the nuts and bolts it should have clear in its mind what it is about. Otherwise only a spindly caricature of evangelism may emerge which brings neither freedom on earth nor rejoicing in heaven. To produce an intelligent, appropriate and Holy Spirit guided strategy for evangelism should be one of the leader's main tasks.

A church does not only need a strategy. It needs to know how to form one and how to keep it under review. This chapter looks at the overall pattern of evangelism and the next chapter at a method whereby a strategy can be worked out.

Most churches give the task of working out a strategy to a small group of people. It may be called a 'mission committee' and it is with this very important group that the leadership of a church seeks to find out God's purposes. The danger of confining evangelism to a small group in this way is that the wider issues of evangelism are sometimes not faced and the group takes its place alongside (or beneath) the finance committee and the women's fellowship. The intention should be that the whole life of the church is permeated with a longing to communicate God in all his fullness to the community, and this may not be best done by one group among others. It is better to engage the whole church in the debate and the decisions. This may be achieved by church weekends devoted to the subject, time for the church committee[1] to discuss it, or material for house groups and a series of sermons.

The strategy which a church adopts will depend on its understanding of evangelism. Often a church assumes it knows what evangelism is without thinking it through in theology, practice and prayer. Without this hard thinking and debate it will fail to answer the first and foremost challenge, 'Define your terms'. It is easy for leaders not to undertake this reasoning or to help their congregations to do so. This can lead to 'knee-jerk evangelism' which answers the statement 'We ought to evangelise' with the question 'What ought we to do?', rather than 'What does this mean?'

What is evangelism?

There are endless definitions of evangelism. One of the most used is that agreed upon in 1989 by Anglican Archbishops from around the world:

To evangelise is to make known by word and deed the love of the crucified and risen Christ in the power of the Holy Spirit, so that people will repent, believe and receive Christ as their Saviour and obediently serve him as Lord in the fellowship of his Church.[2]

However, it is not difficult to criticise this definition . . . it is too churchy . . . it sees the relationship between us and God only in terms of repentance and forgiveness . . . it omits any reference to God the Father.

For many years there have been attempts to define evangelism accurately. I am not sure that such a definition is either possible or even necessary. When the endless debates are examined they have more to do with negatives than positives. People may have a stereotype of evangelism which they are determined should be excluded. This caricature is usually of a flashily dressed man with an unreal smile holding a large black Bible and proclaiming the gospel in a way which allows no dissent. Alternatively people are determined that their understanding of the heart of the gospel should be included – it may be social action, instant conversion, a certain eschatological position or whatever.

Defining anything is itself a negative activity – it draws a boundary and says that within this limit everything is evangelism but outside it nothing is evangelism. The words of Pope Paul VI are worth pondering, 'Any partial and fragmentary definition which attempts to render the reality of evangelisation in all its richness, complexity and dynamism does so only at the risk of impoverishing it and even distorting it. It is impossible to grasp the concept of evangelisation unless one tries to keep in view its essential elements.'[3]

It is better to explain rather than define. At root evangelism is an attitude rather than an activity, and can no more be readily defined than any other attitude such as patriotism or disgust. An evangelistic church is not one involved in a welter of evangelistic activities but one which thinks outwards. The leader will be primarily trying to ensure that there are certain patterns of evangelistic thinking in the church rather than whipping the congregation into a lather of guilt or organising a blizzard of events.

The explanation of evangelism is best done by a series of statements. These may well form the basis of a church's teaching. Some may put greater emphasis on some elements than on others but within the church there is widespread acceptance of the following:

1. Evangelism is addressed to individuals.

A bulletin in a war-torn country stating that 'Peace has been agreed' is good news. For some it may be literally life-saving, for others it is only peripheral to their main concerns. Good news is for everyone, whether they have an obvious need or not.

Evangelism must address a need, but that may not be a classic call to repentance. Instead it may be helping people to realise that in God there are resources which we do not have and that only in relation to him are we whole.

Therefore for the leader to join with a congregation in perceiving where lies the golden thread by which the grace of God touches the need of each human being is one of the most important means of forming a strategy. Indeed from his or her pastoral contact with people the leader may well have a wider knowledge than many of the congregation.

2. Evangelism is addressed to communities.

God in Christ speaks not just to us in our personal lives but also in our lives together. The group may be a school, a hospital, an office or a home. It may be a country or a continent. It may be the whole human race or the whole planet. A local church collecting money for the victims of a disaster is sending gospel to them – for what they need most is food and shelter. The church may also be putting the gospel into words when some members of the congregation speak reconciliation into the divisions in the staff room of a local school.

'Go therefore to all nations and make them my disciples . . .'[4] is not addressed to nation states such as Germany or Brazil. Such a concept was not yet born in New Testament times. *Ethnos* means 'a culture' or 'a community'. We are asked to interpenetrate each culture with 'shalom' – God's peace and righteousness.[5]

Part of the ministry of any church is to hold up a mirror to the culture which surrounds it. It is difficult, for culture is the water we swim in, the pervasive influence on how we talk, how we dress, how we relate to others. Jesus was much misunderstood and much hated because he questioned the axioms of his day about the Sabbath, about attitudes to the state, about their approach to God. The ways of the Kingdom were radically different from thought patterns accepted as 'normal' by his hearers. The church is involved in the process of 'conscientiatisation' in which people become aware of what they have previously taken for granted. The process is usually confined to oppressed groups such as women, blacks and the disabled, but it should not be confined to these. All parts of society need to examine their presuppositions.

3. Evangelism is by both word and action.

Paul spoke scornfully of a 'mere words' statement of the gospel.[6] It is both shown and spoken. The most proclamatory presentation of the gospel cannot fail to have its social implications as those addressed work out what being a Christian entails, and a follower of Christ cannot 'give a cup of cold water' in Christ's name without stating something of the nature of the gospel by that action. The emphasis will change but the diagram is not like this . . .

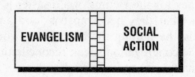

but like this . . .

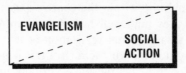

Every action will have a different proportion of social action and proclamation but it can never be entirely one or the other.

4. Evangelism is an act of the Church.

No evangelism can be divorced from its roots. An evangelist is inevitably a member of the Church; the message he or she preaches is one formed within the tradition of the Church, and those who respond become in their turn members of the Church and are brought into its fellowship through baptism. Even the plethora of para-church groups that grow up on the boundaries of the church are made up of members of the church and cannot exist without it.

5. Evangelism should seek the whole of Christian initiation for individuals.

There has always been the danger that the Church has offered 'cheap grace' – that frightening make-believe gospel identified by Bonhoeffer which offers a gospel without cost, a cross without pain. Until recently surprisingly little work had been done on the theological and practical content of Christian initiation. William Abraham sees evangelism in terms of initiation into the Kingdom of God.[7] David Pawson speaks of the need to hold together repentance, faith, baptism and the receiving of the Holy Spirit.[8] Felicity Lawson would add to those four elements being part of the fellowship of the Church and the acceptance of God the Father as Abba and Creator.[9] There has been much questioning of the simple evangelical 'conversion' experience which says that all that people need is the ABCD of the gospel – Admit you are a sinner, Believe that Jesus died for you, Count the cost of discipleship and Decide to follow

him. That may well be exactly the right message for those who
have been brought up within the church – they know the facts
of the gospel, they may well have been baptised – now they
need to come to a personal realisation of it in their lives and
ABCD is a useful guide for them. But this is not a full gospel.
When the majority of people have virtually no knowledge of
the content of the Christian faith and have had no connection
with the Church at any time in their lives then repentance and
faith is not the whole of initiation. The central questions which
those in local churches have to answer are:

(a)   Have those who *are* within the Church come to a position
      of repentance and faith? Many are 'passengers who should
      be pilgrims'.[10] They need to be evangelised by having the
      opportunity to be challenged to accept for themselves
      those things which they know intellectually.

(b)   Is evangelism truly trinitarian? Evangelism can too often
      be seen as 'opening your heart to Jesus'. Where the people
      evangelised know the Christian faith this may be no more
      than a convenient if theologically inexact description of
      repentance and faith. Where there is not this knowledge
      then a Christian message which concentrates upon the
      second person of the Trinity will lead to a commitment
      which can be severely deficient.

(c)   What part does the Holy Spirit play in initiation? For
      many involved in the Charismatic renewal the 'baptism in
      the Spirit' is part of initiation.[11]

(d)   Is evangelism balancing the objective and the subjective
      elements? The basic fact is that 'You did not choose me: I
      chose you'.[12] If all is made to depend on human response,
      evangelism becomes not a proclamation of the majestic
      goodness of God but a pleading for a human change of
      will or, even worse, the manipulation of human beings
      towards a desired response.

Leaders will have to ensure that a whole gospel is being offered
and that the methods used are appropriate to the people con-

cerned. There is little doubt that one of the central debates of the Decade of Evangelism will be the nature of Christian initiation. It may need noticing that the position in the United States is not the same as Western Europe. There ninety-five per cent believe in God, forty-two per cent of the population are in church on any Sunday and two-thirds regard themselves as active members of a church. In Europe the figures are much lower and there is not the same basic knowledge and church membership. Therefore the simple 'repentance and faith' appeal which may be appropriate in the US may not be sufficient in Europe, and evangelistic models from the US may not be wholly appropriate here.

6. Evangelism must have integrity.
A church which seeks holiness and which itself is under the gospel is evangelising. An emphasis on this prevents any thought that evangelism is from the 'elect' to the 'benighted heathen'. It is rather, in the famous sentence, 'one beggar telling another where he can find bread'. Part of this integrity is a readiness to listen and be vulnerable to the people who are evangelised. It is difficult to avoid the word *agape*. Much overused though it may be, there is no better description of the right attitude for the evangelist. This love described in 1 Corinthians 13 cannot, by its very essence, be rude or overbearing, selfish or conceited. It will delight in truth wherever it is found and will go on hoping to the end. It excises humbug. It is plainly ridiculous to say to one's neighbour, 'This week we have a mission and I love you in the name of Christ, but next week the mission is over and I will cease to love you . . .'. Love can have no part in hit-and-run raids or in an evangelism which is impersonal.

7. Evangelism must help people along all the pathways which the Holy Spirit uses to lead people to faith.
The stories of people who have become Christians show that there is no simple route to faith. Surprisingly little research has

been done on these experiences. The Alister Hardy Institute
has collected 5000 stories of 'religious experiences'.[13] Churches
Together in England, with the assistance of the Bible Society,
are involved in a research project to find out what people
experience.[14] It is already clear that while faith is a crisis event
for some, it is a process for others. Some have a sudden date-
able experience while others may have a gradual unfolding over
years, months or weeks. Some initial research suggests that
sixty per cent of Christians claim to have had a process experience. There is some evidence that the older people are the
more likely it is that their experience of faith will be a process.[15]
Therefore an approach to evangelism which looks only for a
sudden experience will not be true to the glorious variety of
the ways the Holy Spirit works. Most evangelical models of
evangelism tend to look for a sudden experience, while non-
evangelicals are inclined to look for a process. Neither is true
to all of what God does.

8. Evangelism means pain.
Any true Christian ministry will have about it a touch of the
cross. For individual Christians it means the pressure of
exposure to the world and the demands of the needy.

But there is also the corporate pain of the church. Evangelism almost always means dropping other parts of the programme so that it can become part of the normal life of the
church. It is as true about an organisation as about D.I.Y.
that 'bits which are tacked onto the outside soon drop off'.
Evangelism can be the flavour of the month but if it is to be
permanent it has to become a normal part of the church life.
Evangelism is risky and costly – and it will soon become clear
that there are much more comfortable things to do. Evangelism
also means the pain of growth with all the difficulties which
that entails.

In practice a church seldom settles down to work out all
the problems associated with evangelism before it starts

evangelising. The normal pattern is for a church to do something, have limited success and then start looking fully at what
it has already done and the principles which lay behind it.

The first thing which needs to be established is the vision.
The leaders of a church must be agreed on this and it is upon
their judgement that it depends. A prophet may prophesy, a
situation may demand action, someone may have a bright idea
– but in the end it is the leaders who have to discern the right
way forward.

The vision

I come as a learner, with no policy to advocate, no plan
already formed to follow. But I come with one burning
desire: it is that in all our activities, sacred and secular and
ecclesiastical and social, we should help each other fix our
eyes on Jesus making him our only guide . . . pray for me
that I may never let go of the unseen hand of the Lord Jesus
and live in daily fellowship with him.

William Temple said that when he was enthroned as Bishop of
Manchester. He had no plan but he had a vision, which was
far more important.

Vision is a mixture of emotion, intellect and determination.
A vision for evangelism will mix a longing to evangelise, an
understanding of what is being done, and the will to put it into
practice. Without any of these three elements there will be no
full vision. No emotion produces a grim evangelism without
sparkle and life. No understanding produces a thoughtless activism. Lack of determination produces many plans but no
action. Vision fires the imagination and starts people thinking
and acting.

Vision will lead on to planning. This is inevitable because
there are many options. Infinite choice produces infinite uncertainty and absolute immobility. Options must be narrowed

down, but there must be consideration of many possibilities. The tendency of many organisations is to see only one course of action and then implement it. This is seldom right. Questions need to be asked, 'Are there alternatives?', 'What is the rationale behind that course of action?' All too often the good becomes the enemy of that best which must be God's will for the church. If this is not sought then the church becomes victim of the last book that one of the leaders has read, the last conference attended, or the last stirring address.

Vision can never be the possession of only one person. It may well begin as the suggestion or the idea of one individual but it cannot remain there or the initiative will fail. Inspiring, encouraging and passing on vision is one of the main tasks of leadership. However it has to be said that Christian leadership is often strong on vision and fails to take the vital next step of linking the vision with what has to be done. As someone cynically said of a preacher, 'He is full of vegetable sermons – full of "let us's" '. The Christian world has bred many conferences of church leaders who have thought rich thoughts, passed detailed resolutions and then found that nothing has happened because nobody has arranged what needed to be done and who was responsible for making sure that something happened.

Most groups find it helpful to have some sort of Gantt Chart process. This determines the goal and then works backwards so as to specify the actions which have to be taken to achieve it, paying close attention to the areas which are particularly difficult. There is no mystery about it. When we go on a car journey we follow the same process. We know our destination so we pick on the best route taking into consideration roadworks and rush hour traffic and the like. This process is sometimes called Critical Path Analysis. It may seem a rather grand term for an everyday process of thought but most people find that the idea of putting the planning process on a chart is helpful. It is easier to visualise. Leaders may need to remember that they are likely to be more conceptual in their thinking than people in the church who may well find diagram and picture more helpful. A simple chart of the following form which plots action to be taken against time can be a useful aid:

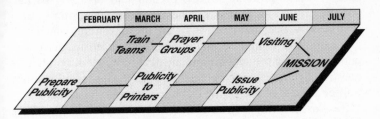

To some this may seem rather cold-blooded, even unspiritual, but if we are setting out to build a church we would expect the architect to turn up with some plans. We would distrust someone who looked to the inspiration of the moment for his ideas on how to spend our money. The original inspiration for the building may have been God-given, but that does not absolve us of the thinking and work which must follow. Richard Lovelace has stern words for those who fail to plan: 'to relinquish the guiding and superintending function of the intellect in our experience seems pious at first, but in the end this course dehumanises us by turning us into either dependent robots waiting to be programmed by the Spirit's guidance, or whimsical enthusiasts blown about by our own hunches and emotions'.[16]

The downside of strategy

A strategy has problems as well as advantages. It is more effective and, in the long run, quicker if these are worked through at the beginning. Too often a vision and a procedure for reaching it are put forward with much enthusiasm and vigour by its proponents and it is left to others to point out the complications which are involved. It is sad to see the enthusiasts wilt and eventually despair as their brain-child is drowned in bucketfuls of cold water. It is better to discover, define and find answers to obstacles beforehand, and any visionary group needs to have someone who is prepared to say, 'Let us find out the problems'. It may not be a popular suggestion, but it is necessary because it means that the questions which will inevitably and rightly be asked have been faced by the group putting forward the scheme and answers have been found. This questioning often has to be begun by the leader for others may well be fearful of appearing to be less than enthusiastic.

Besides, to bring a strategy before a wider audience without having done the necessary homework suggests that the whole is half-baked, and those who do not share the enthusiasm of the inner group feel that they are being asked to buy 'as seen' – where there are suspected deficiencies but they are not being disclosed. If it is felt that a suggestion is not sufficiently robust to be criticised there will be a lack of trust in the whole and the acceptance of any plan of action depends upon trust – firstly in the people who are putting it forward and secondly in the scheme itself.

It is helpful for leaders to categorise the various kinds of difficulty any thinking about the future is likely to encounter. They fall into three groupings:

Material. Often this centres around finance, but it may be lack of suitable buildings or equipment. For the leader these are often the easiest problems to discover. The difficulty is easily stated, something concrete can be suggested as a solution and action can be taken and readily monitored. However Christians can at times be too heavenly minded and fail to take these stumbling blocks seriously enough. The sense that it is 'unspiritual' to take money and practical matters seriously runs deep, and can be a sign of a church which fails to be incarnational. Being truly immersed in the real life of any community will show the importance of practical encouragement as well as words. Christ was blamed for being too earthy by the religious people of his day, and we may need to share his reproach.[17]

People. How people will react to a vision is less easy to discern. Most kinds of strategy require a group of people who are prepared to give considerable time and effort to its implementation. It depends upon the commitment of those concerned. All ministers know the feeling of being let down as people fail to carry through what they have promised. However they may not be aware that laypeople often complain about the lack of commitment of their minister. They often voice feelings about a minister who starts something going, leaves it to laypeople to carry out, loses interest in it and starts something else. Leaders who fail to carry through what they have initiated soon lose the trust of others who understandably will not show much zest for any further schemes.

Spiritual. Hardest to define, yet the most important. If a church does not have spiritual reserves it is unlikely that anything will succeed and all that will be left will be the hulks of past failures – half-built towers which are monuments to what might have been. In mission this is often the foremost area of potential difficulty. If people are not sufficiently enthusiastic about the gospel, are not friends with non-churchgoers in the community and are not prepared for the hard slog of prayer then it is unlikely that it will succeed. For many leaders looking at their congregations there may be a sinking of their hearts. But there is hope. Often the planning and the prayer beforehand and the challenge of the community will begin to raise the spiritual temperature of the church. That is why so many say after a time when a church has concentrated upon mission, 'We don't know what it did for others, but it did us a power of good'.

It will be found that tabulation is often a useful method of recording difficulties. Write down under each of the headings what problems you are likely to encounter – and opposite put the possible answers. If these are not clarified in this way it is likely to cause a sense of unease which is produced by a miasma of uncertainty about the whole affair. In this, as in other areas of leadership, 'naming the demons' is important.

This procedure also enables leaders to be aware of those areas where they do not have any answers. Some difficulties can be overcome easily, some may prove more intractable. But there will be some blanks on the chart of difficulties – areas where there are no apparent solutions. Budgetary needs may seem unattainable; the responses of people cannot be predicted until much later. It is in these areas that faith and reality need to meet. There is a tendency to say 'Jehovah-jireh'[18] and go ahead without further thought. Or it may be that the difficulties suggest that this is not God's plan at all. Alternatively it can happen that a new and better pattern emerges from the ruins of the old. One church had a group of leaders who produced a grandiose scheme for pulling down their church and building something which would be more useful. After long discussion they realised that the difficulties were God's way of directing them to something different, and they recognised that they could realise all their aims and more by a reordering of their present building at a fraction of the cost and trouble of the previous idea.

Exercise

Before getting down to the practical questions which are raised in the next chapter it is useful to check:

1. Are people working to a model of evangelism which concentrates only on individuals . . . or social needs . . . or the environment? Is it rooted in the church?
2. Does the appeal to the individual for conversion embrace other pathways of the Spirit than a sudden 'decision for Christ'?
3. Is there an unwillingness to accept the pain – of hard thinking, of assumptions challenged and of listening to others?

5

Strategy for Evangelism – II

Leaders can spend much time cogitating without coming to any conclusions. Often this is because the basic questions have not been answered. A strategy is a mixture of hard work and the inspiration of the Spirit. This chapter sets out the hard work which needs to be done.

The list of questions which follows has been used in many churches and been found useful in developing a strategy for mission. Indeed it is often in the answering of these questions that the inspiration comes, though leaders need to be careful not to jump to conclusions when only a superficial survey has been made. Each section of the chapter begins with the questions to be asked and is followed by a commentary upon them.

These questions need to be gone through by the leaders, by the church committee and by as many other people as possible. If the congregation is aware of the questions which have been answered they will be far more ready to accept any changes which the strategy may entail. Indeed leaders need to be prepared to see God's pattern come through a 'non-leader'. In a church I was serving many of us cudgelled long in thought and prayer to find where God wanted us to go – in the end it was an elderly, mentally-retarded woman who stood up and said, 'We need something big, something soon': she was absolutely right.

The atmosphere in which the enquiry takes place is all important. It needs to dance with the joy of the gospel. Too many strategies seem to be concocted by grey people for a grey world and to deny life rather than affirming 'life in all its fullness'.[1]

Someone said, 'Evangelism cannot happen by a policy of drift – we have to mean business, but let us not get too grim about it'.

Second, the aim of the enquiry has to be kept in view. Sometimes the answering of the questions becomes an end in itself, particularly if it throws up interesting results as it usually does. The aim is a statement of strategy.

This policy statement can be comparatively short. It is a vision for the future – a 'what might come to pass'. It does not need to be complex or detailed. Above all it needs to come out of what the minister and the congregation have found to be God's will. In too many churches which are seeking to find a policy the minister appears like Moses from the mountaintop and is then mortified when the people fail to recognise the tablets of stone as being the true word of the Lord. There is a danger in saying, 'I am going into retreat for a few days to hear what God is saying to us'. It will be difficult for others to gainsay the resulting declaration for it is seen as coming from a high and holy place, and to oppose it is to oppose God himself. It may well be right for the minister – or, better still, the leaders in the church – to go away for prayer and discussion, but they must not come back and assume that all will automatically accept it or that it cannot be improved by further consultation.

Q.1 (a) *What is the church's policy on evangelism?*
     (b) *If there is a policy:*
          (i)   *has it a 'bias to the excluded'?*
          (ii) *how many in the church know what this policy is
                – and do they agree with it?*
          (iii) *when was its effectiveness last evaluated?*

I have often asked a group which has come together to discuss outreach, 'What is your policy for evangelism?' It is an embarrassing moment. Sometimes the minister shuffles on his chair and the congregation look bemused. Not only is there no policy but no one has ever thought that there ought to be one. Alternatively the minister looks self-satisfied and the others look mystified: only the minister knows what the policy is. There is no use in that. If leaders are thought to be acting in accordance with a hidden agenda there is bound to be suspicion. People fear that things are afoot which they are not privy to, and the resulting lack of trust will destroy any thought of progress.

But it can be that the policy is known but is not accepted. Indeed the very idea that there should be evangelism in the community may be dismissed. The symptoms are clear – only a handful come to meetings about mission, few contribute when the subject is brought up in the church committee, and even fewer are around when anything needs to be done. It is seldom that there is a conspiracy of people who have determined to sabotage the policy, though it may seem so to the leadership when it is being paranoid. Rather it is that most have decided that this is not for them. If this rejection exists, then it may well be best to go back to the beginning with teaching about evangelism, an attempt to involve as many as possible in answering the basic questions and the evolution of a new policy which is truly owned by the congregation.

It is fashionable to talk about any action in the church needing a 'bias to the poor'. It is undeniable that the Bible favours the widow and the fatherless, the 'stranger who is within your gates' and the 'little ones'. In any community faced with the gospel there are the poor – those who are the 'excluded'. They may be very diverse groupings. They can be those from the council estate or bed-sit land who are materially as well as spiritually poor. But the 'excluded' may also be the seriously rich whose semi-mansions are approached by no member of the church. It can be the 'incomers' in a village which does not welcome them, or the young people who cannot fit the staid ways of the church. Leaders will be wise to write down a list of those who are apparently out of touch with the local church and keep it in a prominent position during the whole enquiry. It is all too easy to forget them, and concentrate on those who are familiar and 'think as we think'. The subsidiary question which needs to follow is not, 'Why don't they come to us?' but, 'How are we stopping them coming and how can we go out to them?'

It is sometimes seen as being unspiritual to discuss the effectiveness of what is happening in the church. It is true that we are called to have steadfastness whatever the results. Indeed this is a reflection of the *chesed* of God – that Hebrew word for which Miles Coverdale had to invent a new English word, 'loving-kindness', to describe the patient care of God for his people. But perseverance is not the same as stubborn foolishness. If a policy does not seem to be advancing the Kingdom of God it needs to be looked at again, and possibly abandoned or altered. For example, one church had concentrated on its teenage work and many resources, including a part-time worker, were put into it. But an evaluation showed that few young people came to the social gatherings the church held, and even fewer became active Christians. Meanwhile work with young adults, which was far more promising, was starved of resources. There were those in the church who wanted its limited resources to continue to be directed to the young people since they were said to be the 'seedcorn of the church', while others wanted more help to be given to the many young families in the area. After much debate the latter course was followed. It was a courageous decision for most churches would have tried to stretch resources to cover both areas of work and ended up by doing neither well.

All work in the church needs this kind of evaluation from time to time, and it should be seen, not as an inspection, but as an expression of the way in which the church cares for its people. However kind church leaders may be personally, it is easy for an organisation which they lead to be harsh. There is little love in a church which allows its members' energies to be tied up in failing organisations, fruitless meetings and unproductive endeavours. It can only lead to a joyless discipleship and eventually to the dwindling and death of faith.

Q.2   *In the community in which you are situated:*
    (a) where do people meet?
    (b) what are their main motivations and concerns?
    (c) how much basic Christian knowledge has each age group?
    (d) what is the image of the church in the neighbourhood?

The first question tried to see what sort of policy, if any, there was already. The second begins to evolve a new strategy, and starts, not with the church but with the community in which it is situated. For most churches this means those people in the immediate geographical neighbourhood of the church. But for some 'the community' may be those working in the industrial plants or the businesses which surround the church and are thronged on weekdays, or a university campus or military installation.

There is no substitute for a good map of the neighbourhood. A church needs to be aware of its locality before it can evangelise and it needs to know the prisons and the hospitals, the pubs and the clubs, the schools and the factories which make up the community. I have found that many are curiously ignorant of their surroundings. They may well be aware that there is a school down a certain road but do not know whether it is primary or secondary, still less how large it is or what its standard of religious education is. Often to talk about an area can be a sharing of ignorance and it is useful if someone has done some mild homework finding out the facts – otherwise endless wrangles can take place as to how many go to the bingo hall or what kind of Muslim worships in the mosque. It has been found that a sheet of statistics can save much argument. A few phone calls and a visit to the public library can be all that is required to compose the document.

When thinking about what makes people tick it is easy to be uncharitable. To say of the local young people, 'All they are interested in is smashing the place up' is too sweeping. They may well give generously to charities like Comic Relief and be prepared to spend their spare time helping others. We have to be aware of what people are interested in. One minister in a mining area joined the local angling club, partly because he enjoyed fishing but mainly so that he could meet the men. Many church leaders find that it is not only therapeutic for themselves but also gives an invaluable bridge into the community to follow the local football club or for a woman to join the Townswomen's Guild. It may well be best on such occasions not to hide one's connection with the church. Despite the usually gentle banter people are glad to see those from the church doing something 'normal' and often approach them with a problem. One minister in Liverpool who had returned from a long period abroad as a missionary found that he needed to visit the pantomime and the pubs to find out what his people relished. He frequently brought the cross-talk and the participation of such places into his services and they proved enormously successful, partly because he was talking in a language they could understand and brought a spirituality which was earthed and real.

It is when discussing the concerns of the neighbourhood that it is easy to jump to conclusions. Debt may be a problem. Is the church to set up immediately a debt counselling agency? There is a dearth of things for young mothers to do. Should the church start a meeting for them? Any community has so many needs that churches can leap into action without counting the inevitably limited resources which they have and whether or not this venture is the will of God or just a good idea.

The basic Christian knowledge of local people is an important question. If most people do not know anything about the Christian faith an evangelism which presupposes a knowledge of the facts of the faith is unlikely to be successful. In most areas the extent of this knowledge varies with age. Older people have more residual knowledge than the young and, therefore, are likely to have had both some experience of a local church and more or less solid teaching in their school. Even if it was a long time ago, something has remained. Younger people probably have not had any connection with a church and a multi-faith syllabus at school.[2]

The attitude of local schools to the teaching and practice of religious education is important in this part of the enquiry. Where school assemblies are broadly Christian and convey a sense of the importance of what is being done, and religious education in classrooms is taken seriously, young people will have some groundwork. Where assemblies are uncertain in content and dull in presentation, and religious education puts in front of children a mélange of confused and confusing ideas plucked from many faiths they may be inoculated against 'religion' for life. Churches are often given opportunities of making contact with local schools. Where the chances are well taken it can be significant for the future of evangelism in the area.

Every institution has a generalised image in the mind of those who live around it. Often these images are gross oversimplifications – a school is 'bad', doctors are 'unfriendly', the police are 'good'. Usually these imprecise statements are based on hearsay or on one or two personal experiences. The church is the same. If someone from 'St Agatha's' calls on an evangelistic visit the name will immediately produce these generalisations in the mind of the person being contacted. If they are negative the door will be shut; if they are positive there is a chance for genuine meeting. Churches should not massage their images like politicians but their importance for evangelism is considerable for those who have little contact with the church. The significance of what are sometimes rather dismissively called the 'occasional services' – baptisms, weddings and funerals – cannot be rated too highly. The people concerned are at a momentous hinge-point in their lives and their families have come to support them with sympathy or congratulations. If the church is seen as caring, human and interested in them as people as well as bringing a sense of the eternal into life the image left will persist for years. If the reverse is true an aversion to any approach from the church can last a lifetime.[3]

Q.3   *How does God seem to be working in the present? What*
      means is he using to bring people to himself and who are
      they?

      There are subsidiary questions:

      (a) *What was the main factor which led to their turning*
          to God?

      (b) *Has their conversion been sudden or a gradual*
          unfolding?

      (c) *What proportion of these people have had some sort*
          of Christian upbringing?

The church generally does not learn from those who have
recently become Christians. Their experience gives an up-to-
the-minute indication of how God is working, and yet we ignore
the nuggets of information which they are carrying. God never
repeats his patterns so each story will be unique, but their
cumulative effect displays how the Spirit is working. The
enquiry begins to answer questions about the effectiveness of
past evangelistic methods, about the tortuous pathways which
people tread, and about the background of those who have
recently joined the church. Leaders can too easily be misled by
a single spectacular conversion into thinking that it must be a
blueprint for all.

It has to be the leadership of the church which should undertake this joyful task of asking the newcomers about their spiritual journeyings. Only a few people, possibly only one, can
hold the different stories together, compare them and draw
conclusions. Further those questioned will be more ready to
talk to someone who is known to be in a leadership position
than to an unknown. Thirdly, it is the leadership who will need,
while they are listening to the story of someone's past, to be
seeking what God's next step for them should be.

I find that those who have recently become Christians are
only too willing to talk of something which has come to be very
precious to them. Many have said that it has been a spiritually
enlightening thing to do for it meant they were able to review
their life and see how God had been working in the past to

lead them to their present point of commitment. Moreover they are both intrigued and honoured that their story should have such significance that the leadership of the church should be interested.

The leader needs to have a pattern of questions in his or her mind before embarking on this enquiry. It is helpful to know:

had they some sort of Christian background?
what was their early experience of God?
when did they first become aware of the presence of God in their lives?
how far have other people influenced them?
what was the main factor which led them closer to God?
what part of the gospel message had the greatest impact on them?
how has their view of God changed?
how has their lifestyle been altered?
whether they had a sudden or gradual experience of God?
what their experience of entering the church was like? (There may be some salutary shocks here.)

Those approached will not necessarily be just those people who have come for adult confirmation or baptism. There will be those who have just started coming to church, with no particular sign of deeper commitment. There will be young people who have come back from college with a matured and lively faith. It also needs to include those who seem to be becoming less consistent after a burst of enthusiasm for God and his people: negative reactions are, if anything, more helpful than positive.

The answers should lead to many insights into mission. It may include some further far-reaching questions. It was clear in one church I visited that over a third of the congregation were recent adult converts with no previous experience of any church. They had not been to Sunday School or had any Christian education. They had come from the 'outside'. But the church, like those of most denominations, assumed that people had a basic knowledge of the Bible and the church's year and how the church operated. But this was not true of a third of the congregation. They had no idea what a 'diocese' was, let alone a 'deanery synod'. Their lack of scriptural background meant that they could not put into context the sermons they heard: some, despite being avid readers of the Bible, did not know the difference between the Old and the New Testaments. They did not know the significance of Advent or what an Anglo-Catholic was. Many were only kept going by the warmth of their experience of Christ. They felt they had wandered into a place where everyone except themselves knew what was happening. The church, when they realised the situation, laid on an 'induction course' to enable them to learn the Bible and some of the less destructive aspects of ecclesiasticism.

It is often found that the answers to such an enquiry appear to solve almost automatically the wider questions about evangelism. If it is found, as is usual, that most people have had a long and gradual unfolding of God it is clearly unwise only to use evangelistic methods which look for a sudden conversion. If the healing ministry has been important in the conversion of many then it will need greater emphasis. If membership of a particular organisation or group has been useful then it needs further encouragement. Indeed there is a danger that people assume that merely asking newcomers about their spiritual journeys automatically produces an evangelistic strategy. It has to be remembered that they are individuals with their own quirks and preferences – they are not totally representative. They can provide clues as to where the answers are to be found but are not the complete solution.

There may be more subtle results. It may be that the love of God has been the part of the gospel which spoke to many – if so it suggests both that this aspect of the gospel should be underlined and that an absence of love may be part of the milieu of the neighbourhood. It will also be found that people's journeys are not over. Several may be undertaking a parallel exploration: it may be a desire for silence and contemplation, or a hunger to experience the power of the Holy Spirit, or a wish for more theological understanding. On such insights the future policy of the church can be based.

One minister who had done this exercise reported that all the people he had asked had had what seemed to me to be a remarkably uniform experience of God. We discussed it more deeply and it was clear that he had tried to force the story of each individual into his own 'plan of salvation'. We have to have integrity and allow God's Holy Spirit to speak to us through these people without prejudging what the message is going to be.

Q.4   *Do the structures of the church help or hinder evangelism?*
Many modern churches evolve a two-bodied structure.

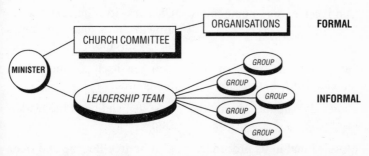

The formal part of the structure is probably older than the informal. Some of it will be required by denominational rules, especially where the raising and expenditure of money are concerned. The gaggle of much more loosely structured groups is probably of recent growth. In many churches they will have been added onto the formal layer with the result that many churches with this dual structure are extraordinarily busy, for members are involved in both running the organisations and attending groups. It may leave them with little time for mission. Some churches seem like 'black holes' which suck in the energies of their members to such an extent that nothing escapes to encourage and evangelise the world. While it would be illegitimate to push the analogy too far the 'event horizon' of a black hole (from inside which no light can escape) well describes the point at which a church becomes so busy that exhaustion is its main characteristic, and evangelism is impossible because nothing can be done outside the life of the church.

Certain differences between a group and an organisation are important. These distinctions cannot be pressed too hard for a group can turn into an organisation and vice versa at different times in its life. For example a group can decide to have a time of self-audit and planning which is more appropriate to an organisation. However they are generally true.

Organisation	Group
Resistant to change	More capable of change
Can receive large numbers	Changes its character when growth takes place (becomes an organisation)
Sees itself as part of the 'official' church structure	Can see itself as apart from the church
Demands support from the leadership	Less demanding of the leadership
More formal in its procedures	Can be free-flowing and open to change (though it can fossilise)
Often run by a committee	Leadership is often 'charismatic' – based on personality of individuals
Has established communication lines with the church leadership	Communication often less organised – and sometimes not wanted
Likely to be long-lived	Are often founded, flourish and die within a short time

Death can be difficult	Death more expected and less traumatic

There are three areas which have to be addressed.

1. Are the existing organisations the right ones?

On the moors in North Yorkshire there are many standing stones – great monoliths stark against the sky. What they were put there for can only be guessed at . . . grave stones of prehistoric man . . . medieval boundary markers . . . sites of ancient worship. Organisations in churches can have the same character. They stand there, their purpose lost in the mists of parish history, relics of past enthusiasms and previous movements of the Holy Spirit. One church I visited had twenty-eight different organisations. The whole effort of the church was taken up in keeping these afloat. One question has to be asked of every organisation – what is God's will for you? For some it may be a decent funeral, for some it may be a change in emphasis, for others it will mean expansion and new life.

2. Is the overall pattern of organisation and groups correct?

Each individual part of the structure may be functioning well, but the overall effect can be stifling. There are many healthy plants but their cumulative effect is to strangle each other. In a garden it is sometimes necessary to thin out good plants so that others have room to grow. The leadership must look at the overall effect of the structure on the members of the congregation. If they spend all their time servicing the church as an organisation they will have no time for their families and no time for their mission to the world. The ratio between the number of organisations/groups and the numbers in the congregation probably should not be more than one to fifteen: i.e. ten groups/organisations in a congregation of 150.

3. Do the structures look outwards?

Structures are erected by people within the church, and so are inevitably those which best suit themselves. They are not necessarily right for those outside and in a church which is committed to mission each part of the structure has to be judged by that criterion. The challenge of thinking outwards has to be put to each part of the church. I was much moved by watching a group of elderly women meeting in their 'Women's Fellowship'. Their committee had decided they needed to look outwards, and greatly daring they had decided to drop the time-honoured pattern of 'a speaker, a prayer and a cup of tea'. They had invited four equally elderly ladies from a nearby church to talk about prayer. The four were petrified: none had ever spoken before in public. The first spoke, haltingly but sincerely, for about three minutes. The second started, and, within a minute one of the home group chipped in, 'That's just what I find when I pray'. A free for all broke out as they all started to talk about what prayer meant to them and its difficulties and joys. The meeting effervesced as their own experience was heard and honoured. After a time it quietened down and someone said, 'How can we teach all this to our grandchildren and our friends?' and they were away on a long discussion on a form of mission that all of them were capable of.

Groups also can be like records stuck in a groove – the same opinions and prayers delivered by the same people in the same words week after week. The work of the leadership of the church in these situations is to act as a 'group doctor' and prescribe a determined look outwards. Often this means looking at the life of each member *outside* the group and discerning how the group can help the witness of that person at home and at work. It may mean discussing the ethical issues with which each is faced, praying for them in difficult times, making practical suggestions as to how the Bible can give light to their situation.

Q.5 *Have the evangelists in the church been identified? Are they being: set free . . . trained . . . affirmed . . . encouraged . . . used?*

All Christians are called to be witnesses and to tell the two unique stories which they know – the story of Jesus Christ and the story of what he has done in their lives. But there are some who are particularly gifted by the Holy Spirit as evangelists. These are those who are able to speak naturally about Christ and, above all, bring others to a point where they want to discover more for themselves and entrust themselves to God.[4] They are an essential gift of God to the church, and they must be honoured.

But this is not always easy. Evangelists are people on the edge. They are often strongly individualistic, even egotistic. They are impatient of structures, and not prepared to wait while ecclesiastical wheels grind slowly through committees and consultations. They can be difficult to control and unwilling to be part of a structure. The person of St Paul is a good example of this. He had a burning desire to evangelise – if the church in Jerusalem wanted to keep him under control, so much the worse for them. He was not an easy companion and quarrelled with his fellow-workers on at least two occasions. He wanted things done his way and had a drive about him that meant that others were either swept up in it or they were disregarded. He had little time for weakness – Mark had failed once and so could not be trusted again. People found that they could not be neutral about him – you either loved him deeply or found him intolerable. With those in the churches he had founded he was tenderness itself as long as they kept to the ways he had laid down, but he was far from patient with those who strayed. Such is the nature of an evangelist.

If one had to generalise the evangelist is someone who operates outside the structure and so is in deep personal need of affirmation. It can be a lonely ministry. Many full-time evangelists find that the glamour of the public platform soon wears thin, and sub-Christian motivations easily creep in. If nobody else will affirm me I will affirm myself by proclaiming, not Christ, but my own worth and personal power and how many people I have influenced for Christ. It has to be said that this lack of self-confidence comes often not from the personal needs of the evangelist but from the church which has failed to own and honour their ministry. But this common scenario does not make it easy for the church to give the appropriate support, and there can be a stand-off situation where the church say, 'We will recognise you if you come within our structures' and the evangelist says, 'I want to be recognised for who I am, without conforming to your stereotype'. Not surprisingly the church has had difficulty with the evangelist. They do not fit into a parish system because for them, 'The world is my parish'.[5]

All denominations have had difficulty in discovering, training, accrediting and using evangelists. While they minister in the local church the problems are not so obvious. They can be honoured and used, but if they find that they operate more widely the difficulties may be acute. The Church of England is typical – it has set up commissions, suggested an Order of Evangelists but failed to come up with a solution.[6]

Evangelists need to be used. They often have great ideas – even grandiose ones. They have an inner urge which needs to be fulfilled. It may be of the Holy Spirit or it may be of their own nature – more often it is a mixture of the two.[7] Freed from the administration of the church they need to be able to experiment, to venture and to be allowed to fail.

And they need training and support. Once again it is 'on the job' training which is most appropriate. They need one or two people they can throw ideas against, with whom they can pray through the future and debrief the past, and whom they can trust and lean upon. The mentor must be honest, not shy to puncture the wildest ideas, prepared to give much praise but also to work through personal weaknesses. This ongoing relationship should continue for years. Alongside this, or in addition to this, the evangelist needs a spiritual director. Evangelists are exposed to more subtle and constant temptations than the usual. They have few constant factors in their lives, live under pressure and on the move. It is not easy to develop a pattern of prayer in a life which lacks structure, or to remain close to Christ in his humility when crowds adulate at one time and ignore or threaten at another.

Q.6 *Are people praying so that they can hear the guidance of*
      God – and if God says 'Go' does anything happen?

Evangelism is not putting into practice the latest wheeze. It is
aligning our will with that of God almighty so that we join with
him in his mission to the world. That means prayer – not the
sudden burst of panic prayer, but the steady practice of the
presence of God which leads to us having the mind of Christ.
Nowhere else is the leader more under pressure. Surveys have
shown that the first thing which happens when a minister begins
to go downhill is the neglect of prayer. Often I have found that
someone makes a beguiling suggestion which fills the mind and
instead of finding the will of God we come to him and ask, 'Is
this what we ought to do?' It is not the right question. We
should spend time with God and let his suggestion arise in our
mind so that our dreams are his dreams and his plans our plans.

There is a spirituality of evangelism. First there is the quiet-
ening down in his presence. Away go all our plans and our
ideas, and we concentrate, either alone or as a group, on him.
Matthew 6:6 speaks of the need to 'shut the door' when we
come into the Father's presence and this requires the deliberate
and sometimes difficult process of settling the centre of our
being upon him. Sometimes it can take a few minutes, sometimes much longer, but it is essential before we start talking
with him.

Secondly, we need to look at the world with his eyes. Often
this will be thinking and praying for people. We enter into their
situation, feel their feelings, see the future through their eyes.
There is the widower left bereft and terribly alone, finding out
all those things his wife did for him and which he now has to
do for himself: the shopping and the ironing now seem pointless
as well as difficult. There is the young woman who married in
haste and is now learning to repent at leisure . . . left with two
small children and a husband who comes only occasionally.
There is the business man who seems so smoothly successful
on the outside, but one suspects is deeply unsure of himself.
We in prayer enter into their situations before God.

Thirdly, we bring before God ourselves. How far are we really prepared to evangelise in his way? Are we really thinking about a commando raid to bring a few people into the church organisation so that we can say that it has grown? Do we really want evangelism on his terms, which may require a vulnerability which we do not wish for? It may mean changes in the way the church operates which we are fairly sure will upset many regulars, and we would rather not have to do battle even if the Lord is on our side. Fortunately God does not require of us a perfect motive. He demands truth – that we know ourselves and our own hopes and fears. He wants the Christian leader to face up to himself or herself – to know that we are ambitious and want our church to grow, to be aware that we are frightened of that group in the church who seem so sure of themselves, that we are prepared to go forward despite pain, provided it is not too bad. He takes the dross of mixed motives and turns them into gold.

But there is the question of obedience. Is the church prepared for the changes that are called for? Is the leadership willing for the changes in personal attitudes which are demanded? For many leaders the root question is, 'Which is more important – my fear of people or my love for God?' The two are opposites. Just as John speaks of love casting out fear, so fear casts out love.[8] But this does not mean that the fearful leader is useless to God. Through the pages of the Bible there is a catalogue of the fearful – Moses, Jeremiah, Hosea, Peter, Ananias, Paul. Paul speaks for all: 'I came to you in weakness and fear and with much trembling'.[9] No Christian leader can escape fear. Each has his or her own area of fear. Some find speaking so nerve-wracking that I have known people be physically sick before preaching. Others are thrown into despair by criticism, and I have known others lie awake half the night before a meeting of the church committee. Some flinch at the sight of a particular member of their congregation, and others have become so ecclesiasticised that they have become fearful of the world outside the church.[10]

There is nothing wrong in fear – it is a natural human reaction to a threat. That the threat may not be as great as we imagine is no comfort – a noise downstairs in the middle of the night is equally upsetting whether the burglar is real or imagined. Every leader has experienced it, just as every truthful soldier has known it on the battlefield. It is how we deal with it that matters. There are various unhelpful reactions to personal fear:

(a) it paralyses us so that we achieve nothing.

(b) it throws us into a frenzy of activity which is intended to deal with the cause of the fear but which in fact circles it without looking at the cause squarely.

(c) we engage in displacement activity – I have two difficult letters to write: I pick up one and put it down. I pick up the other and put it down. Then I go and make a cup of coffee.

(d) we look for someone to tell us what to do – an authority figure who can share the weight with us.

Or we accept it as part of leadership and realise that it is also going to be part of any church which is on the move.

Leading for Mission

Preparing for mission involves a new look at the whole life of the church, and especially the relationship between the leadership, the rest of the church and people outside the church. This chapter is a study of the types of power which each wield and the relationships between them.

Christian leaders seldom realise they have power. They may be very conscious of the power of others – that self-opinionated person on the church committee, the bishop, the choir, the group which says, 'The Lord has said unto us . . .'. Yet if you ask any member of almost any congregation where power lies, they will nearly always point first to the minister.

It is not only important for leaders to recognise that they have power; they need also to be able to acknowledge it, identify it and see if they are using it legitimately or wrongly. This chapter will give some indications of the kinds of power there are, how they can be exercised helpfully, or otherwise, and the way in which they relate to mission. It is unhelpful if Christian leaders are unaware of the effect they have on others and the types of power they exercise. Often this can be due to an excessive concentration upon the servant model of ministry which speaks much of the powerlessness of Christ and the vulnerability that the Christian leader should have to the church and the world. A look at the life of Christ shows that this is untrue. While there was a powerlessness about the one 'who emptied himself and became as a servant' there was also much power. This was recognised by the crowds he drew to himself, the hostility he aroused in his enemies and the authority which was acknowledged by both friends and enemies. Like it or not Christian leaders have much power. To identify the kinds of power you are exercising is not easy and a 'faithful friend' who can tell you the truth can do much to help.

C. E. B. Cranfield said, 'How extensively does the worldly view of power penetrate and permeate the life of the church. The truth of the saying that "power corrupts" is far too often confirmed in the Church and when spiritual leadership is abused in this way, "the corruption of the best is the worst".' Power gives the opportunity of hurting people. Most ministers do not realise how they can hurt others – indeed are indignant when this is pointed out to them. But the more the power the greater the possibility of damaging another.[1]

Possibly the most useful classification is that of French and Raven which sets out five possible 'types' of power: reward, coercive, legitimate, referent and expert. I have added another – 'spiritual power' – which is as capable of both use and abuse as any other kind of power. It also needs discussing dispassionately to see where the pitfalls lie.[2] One of the greatest values of French and Raven's classification is that it takes into account the attitude of the person who is the recipient of power as well as the position of the person with power.[3] For the sake of simplicity we are speaking about individual Christian leaders. However it may need recognising that institutions have power as well as individuals. A bank has a power different from a bank manager and its procedures and ethos can be ruthless or forbearing, complex or simple. So has a church. As an institution it is not difficult to see when in the past it has been tyrannical or saintly, corrupt or wholesome in its use of power.

Reward power

The subordinate recognises that the person with power can give rewards if he or she does what is wanted. At its most blatant the Christian leader is seen as dispensing or withholding forgiveness. Indeed the biblical view of authority gives warrant for this: 'whosesoever sins you forgive they are forgiven, whosesoever sins you retain they are retained.'[4] Absolution is awesome in its implications. Many refuse to accept the words at face value, wishing to see themselves as declaring the forgiveness which God has given. No doubt this is true, but the ultimate force of our Lord's statement is the negative. To 'retain' sin means leaving people in their guilt. There are certainly times when this is right, when it is thought that repentance is superficial or even fraudulent. But it is not to be taken lightly, not least because it can engender an unwholesome fear of oneself in other people.

But there are lesser but still potent rewards which can be given. To shut someone off from one's company and conversation can be devastating for some. Yet I have known occasions when the minister cuts a member of the congregation dead for some offence. Once again it has to be emphasised that the more the power, the greater the opportunity to hurt. Some are pathetically reliant upon a smile or a friendly word from the minister. This is particularly true after a time of intense counselling. It may be that a crisis has happened in the person's life and much time has been spent together. There has been a close, if rather one-sided relationship. The person has been helped at a time when he has been very vulnerable, and is deeply grateful for the support which has been given. For the minister it has been a purely professional relationship. For the 'client' concerned it has been deeply personal. If the minister tries to go back to the previous rather distant relationship where the person is just another member of the congregation, much hurt can be caused. In his vulnerability the individual wonders why the relationship has changed and become cold and searches himself to see whether his actions have brought about this change. This does not mean that there has been any improper relationship – but it does underline the need for careful weaning to bring the relationship onto a less close footing. It is something that happens at the end of most counselling relationships.

The Christian leader does not only give presents. He or she also receives them. In some churches the reward is monetary. Not common in Europe it is normal in the US: if a church has a good minister they will usually give him a raise, if only to keep him or her out of the hands of another church which will come and offer a better salary.[5] But people reward us also by praise, by accepting our initiatives, by friendliness. These mean a great deal to a minister who is always uncertain how the work is going. If someone is seen to agree with what is happening it is manna to the soul, especially if the leader is in a time of personal uncertainty.

Often rewards of this kind are best accepted graciously, and used as a basis for thanksgiving rather than pride. Having said that, I still have not found the appropriate response to, 'That was a good sermon this morning'. On the rare occasions it has been said to me I have found that 'Praise the Lord' sounds too pious, while 'It is a nice day' is either ungracious or it suggests that one is hard of hearing. 'What was it that particularly struck you?' puts them on the spot, while 'Would you like a full text?' gives more significance to a casual remark than it deserves. Perhaps 'Thank you' is the easiest and best reply.

The dangers of the use of reward power are many. Relationships built upon this last only as long as the rewards are forthcoming. If ministers build their relationships with their congregation upon this mutual 'stroking' then the chaplaincy model of ministry becomes normal – where the minister is there merely to serve the needs of the community, not to lead or inspire.[6]

The dangers of the chaplaincy model are obvious enough, but there are more subtle risks. I went once to a great auditorium in Los Angeles. It had been built to house the crowds which came to hear a certain great preacher. But he was no longer the man he was – on the platform he was a pathetic, elderly figure, trying unsuccessfully to recapture the fire of his youth. The hall was full of echoing spaces. The great congregation had melted away. The preacher of old had built a congregation which depended on him rewarding those who came with a sermon which sent them home with a song in their hearts. The tune had died and the congregation had gone to find a more skilful Pied Piper. He had founded a 'dependency culture' but people had discovered they were no longer dependant on him and so had voted with their feet. The danger of dependency is not confined to the great preacher. It may be the skilled counsellor who gathers around him or her a crowd of people who are, for a time, deeply grateful for their ministrations. It may be a wonder-worker who is expected to produce more and more startling charismatic events.

Some dependency is right. It is impossible in human relationships to exclude a need for each other. But if that becomes the foundation of the relationship then there is much danger.

Coercive power

This is the reverse of reward power. It emphasises the punishment that the powerful person can give rather than the rewards. It appeals to the managerial style that Michael Maccoby called 'the Jungle Fighter' where all in business is red in tooth and claw, and where the winners eat the losers. He distinguished two kinds – the lion who forced his will on others or the fox, who manipulated his will onto others: whichever way is chosen the result is the same.[7]

Clearly it can operate as the deliberate arousal of fear in the minds of the subordinates. The fear of hellfire used to be much more real, and 'dangling them over the pit' was a normal technique in both Evangelical and Catholic circles.[8]

It can be more subtly conveyed by the expressed or suggested threat, 'If you do that, then I'll do this . . .'. Ministers can both do this and have it done to them. Blackmail is never pleasant. The minister who threatens to resign if he does not get his own way, or the organist who deliberately plays badly when she is asked for music she does not like, are both using coercive power. It is never a pretty sight, for it contradicts the servant-hood which should prevail within the church. If a leader is ever tempted in this way he or she needs to search their motivations very carefully. It can be necessary in some extreme situations to take appropriate action, even resignation. But if this is held over the church as a threat beforehand it suggests something wrong is taking place.

There will be those who try to coerce the minister. I had a policy, which I made known, of always accepting every resig-nation which was offered. I did not think it was right for the church to be held to ransom by an individual or a group on the one hand, nor did I want people to offer their resignation without being aware of the consequences.

Legitimate power

The person with power is recognised as having it because of his or her position in the organisation, which is often hierarchical in structure. The minister is looked up to because he or she is ordained. This is emphasised early in their time in a new church. Nearly all denominations have some sort of induction event, like an institution or a licensing which goes out of its way to underline the minister's legitimate power. This is often stressed by the presence of a bishop or superintendent. The minister is given status within the new ministry and the congre-gation is reminded of the fact that he or she has been recognised as a minister of the wider church.

There is nothing wrong in respecting a person because of their position. Even hot-tempered Paul recognised the position of the high priest when he apologised for insulting Ananias, reminding himself of the Scripture which said, 'You shall not abuse the ruler of your people'.[9] While the present day is rightly suspicious of the way in which 'establishment' figures have misused their position in the past the need for sensible, undeferential respect is obvious. If there is no acceptance of the role of the police, the judiciary, the government and the democratic process, chaos is more likely than enlightenment.

But legitimate power can be misused. It is most commonly seen in bureaucracies when the status of the post held by the person concerned is all important. When a tax inspector asks questions of my tax returns, it is the status given to her by the state which is most important. It can lead to the jumped-up jack-in-office so beloved by satirists. J. H. Boren composed a song to the bureaucrat called, 'When in doubt, mumble':

> Implement, finalise, thrust and embue;
> Interface, maximise, meet and review;
> Orchestrate, optimize, test and compute;
> Dialogue, quantify, rate and refute.

Within the church to say, 'You do this because I say so and I am the minister' is disgraceful. It misuses the power which has been given by turning it into an instrument of repression. It is even more dangerous because it may evoke a sinister response. There are some, often because of a poor relationship with their parents, who enjoy being ordered around. It is not a healthy reaction and it should have no part in the church for as Christ himself said of the hierarchical patterns of his day, 'It shall not be so among you'.

Further fantasy can overwhelm reality. Leaders walk hung about with expectations heaped upon them. If they are lay they are supposed to be available to the people, overview some major area of the church's life, meet frequently to pray and plan with fellow-leaders and yet also be good with their family and efficient at their work. The minister is supposed to care for all, preach like Billy Graham, be good with all ages, administer, care and pastor as well as be an evangelist . . . The bishop is expected to head up a complex administrative machinery, look after his clergy, be a spokesperson for the church, evangelise the structures of power in the area, be available to all . . .

There is something profoundly unhealthy in the way the church insists on overloading its leaders. All organisations complain that they burden their leaders with expectations, but the gap between what is expected and what is possible is probably wider in the church than anywhere else. Perhaps it is felt that status within the church requires something more than human, and so we can treat leaders as though they were superhuman. Perhaps it is felt that leadership in the church requires the position of a servant and servants are best kept in their place by being loaded with work. Often there is a degree of unreality – people look for 'a holy man of God'[10] and what they get is the Reverend X with his personality, his gifts and his deficiencies. It should be said here that the position of women is harder. Because they are moving into areas which previously they have not occupied, the expectations have not become settled and so they vary wildly from one person to another – one may be deeply suspicious of all they do, another may see them as standard bearers for feminism, while others tend to pat them on the head. The church should be deeply grateful to those women who are setting the role models which communities of the future will accept as normal – but who are feeling the pain of doing so.

To avoid being shoehorned into this shape marked 'minister' requires a positive determination to be one's own person, to pursue one's own hobbies, and make space for the family. Yet even this has its dangers. There is something profoundly unsettling about the minister who is determined to be 'one of the boys (or girls)'. There is a place for letting one's hair down, but a minister is, like it or not, a representative of the church of Christ and, to many, of Christ himself. The old cartoon showed two men at a bar looking contemptuously at a minister who is knocking back the beer and saying, 'The thing I can't stand about him is his unholier than thou attitude'. Christ had a wonderful ability to go into the places where people were and some were far from respectable. Yet even in the most unsavoury place he kept a calm dignity which drew people to him rather than repell them. It is an attitude which leaders should pray to be able to imitate. Archbishop Derek Worlock spoke on behalf of the Roman Catholic bishops of England and Wales when he asked for encouragement for all theological students 'to move away from the unacknowledged fear of secular society and culture'. The present Pope has asked that priests should be 'heralds of the gospel, who are experts in humanity', because only then could they win the world for Christ.

Referent power

If legitimate power refers to the respect which is due to the office, referent power is respect which is owed to the leader as a person.[11] Often people identify with the leader because of his or her charisma or reputation. At its most adolescent it is wanting to be part of 'X's gang', while at its most mature it is a recognition of someone because they are seen as being people worth respecting. A mature relationship of this kind is no hero-worship, but one based upon a sober knowledge of the other, warts and all.

It is a power which has great possibilities for good or evil. It can be the hypnotic spell that many followers of Hitler spoke of or the 'authority' that Christ had for so many. It may be that its origin is what seems to be the universal human need to worship something or somebody outside ourselves. It can be the most exhilarating and selfless attitude that is possible. However it is said that a baby duck will attach itself to the first moving thing that it sees. If that is its mother, well and good, but if it is a tractor or the farmer's boot it will grow up to be a duck with problems. If something worthy of worship is not found the human psyche will fix itself upon garbage.

If a leader is worthy of respect then his or her referent power will increase with time. They will show a steadfastness and reliability which will reinforce the respect of others. The contrary, of course, is also true. Some ministers may come to a new church with a great reputation but unfortunately closer acquaintance does not lead to greater respect. Nearly always the growth or decline of referent power is built upon integrity. If a person is seen to have this quality they will be respected, and if it is lacking their stock of goodwill will diminish.

Expert power

The person with power is seen as someone with particular expertise. It can be a mechanic looking at a car and saying, 'Well, it's the gasket on the manifold which has gone' or a sociologist wrapping the obvious in obfuscation or the preacher showing how clever he is by quoting half-read theologians. Or it can be the knowledge which enables the scholar to explain the complex in terms which the non-expert can understand, or the preacher who can make ideas live for people. For some reason the term 'populariser' is often seen as derogatory. It should not be so, for in many subjects an even greater skill than attaining knowledge is the ability to explain it to others. It is the skill of a teacher.

There is also something rather pathetic about a Christian leader who uses the skills of yesteryear. The evangelistic methods which were good when he was young are still trotted out though they no longer have any contemporary relevance. The texts which helped someone once are still applied as poultices but bring no relief.

Reliance on this power leads to 'technological relationships'. I may be friendly with my garage mechanic, my dentist and my tax inspector. I need their skills, but our relationship is no deeper than that. Often ministers are disappointed by this. What seemed a close relationship with an about-to-be-married couple or a recently bereaved person turns out to be technological – they needed our skills as a wedding or funeral officiant. The memory of the friendship may well be useful pre-evangelism so that they are more ready to hear the gospel when they next encounter it, but is not itself directly evangelistic.

The right use of power

All people wield power in some aspects of their lives. It may be the power of a mother over her children, the power of a politician over our lives, or the power of a saint of God over the world.

Any leader is likely to wield more than one kind of power. A good leader in scientific research is likely to have both referent and expert power – personal qualities and professional skills. A good sales manager is likely to have referent power as well as legitimate power on the organisation chart of the company. A good minister may well be honoured because he is ordained, respected because he has integrity and have skills in counselling – i.e. possess legitimate, referent and expert power.[12]

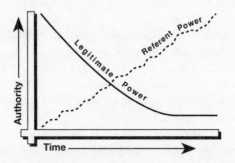

Nor is the relationship between the powers static. One may diminish while another increases. The power wielded by a minister during his or her ministry demonstrates this. At first legitimate power is high – the bishop or superintendent has come and formally inducted the new minister. However people do not know her so her referent power is low. However the impetus given by the hierarchy of the church at the beginning soon loses momentum. If respect for the minister's personal qualities does not grow then soon he or she is going to be left destitute. The danger is that the remaining tatters of legitimate power are seen as the only power left and feeble cries of 'But I am the minister . . .' are heard.

The power exercised will be a mixture of the five powers above. The right use of these powers for a church in mission is essential. The truth of this can often be best demonstrated if one kind of ministry is seen in isolation: for example that of evangelism. That too can be used or misused.

To promise only reward to those who turn to Christ is to prostitute the gospel. To say that the gospel is no more than a promise of a place in the inner fellowship of the church in this life and God's 'well done' in the hereafter is to state only a half-truth. The 'prosperity gospel' which promises material benefits in this life and eternal bliss, but without that counter-balancing strand of the Scriptures and Christian experience which speaks of pain and doubt and suffering for Christ, is a pernicious half-truth.

We may evangelise by coercion -- often by producing guilt. One man said, 'I was taught that a day was wasted if I did not explain the gospel to another person'. After years of attempting this as a young man he realised its futility and turned away from the truth, only returning many years later. Our forefathers preached by 'dangling them over the pit' so that in fear they ran to Christ for salvation.

'This is the tradition of the Church' or 'This is what the Bible teaches' can be sensible statements which reinforce the presentation of the gospel. But they can be 'knock-you-down-arguments' which brook no dissent, using the rightful respect for fountainheads of authority as a manipulative agency. This way lies ecclesiastical or biblical fundamentalism.

On the other hand to misuse the respect which people have for us as people is to betray their trust. If someone says,

'I'd believe anything she says', it puts a great burden on the leader for if she leads them into the Swamp of Despair rather than towards the Glorious City she bears a heavy responsibility.

In the same way to blind people by our real or pretended skills is to complicate the gospel of Jesus Christ so that it is no longer able to be heard by the 'little ones' whom God loves so greatly.

The answer to every abuse of power is love and justice. They cleanse what can be negative. There are those who have argued that all power by one person over another is wrong: these anarchists want to obliterate the ties of the family, the authority of the state and the leadership of the church. They see only the negative side of power. But it does not have to be so. The Kingdom of God must be about power because it is fundamental to human relationships. Only if it is exorcised in the atmosphere of the Kingdom is it tolerable and beneficial.

A reminder from 'Maggie Ross' is a corrective to much twentieth-century thinking about the ministry. While she speaks of clergy, it refers equally well to lay leaders:

> In the very early churches, ministry was not a career; it was not sought after, and the personal conviction that one might have a vocation to be one of the organization's officials carried little weight. In fact, the people who best understood the practical implications of interrelatedness in kenotic love and the dangers of power politics shunned ordination. They had to be hunted down by their bishops, who were forced to kidnap them in order to ordain them.[13]

Exercise

A. Derek Sheane (of I.C.I.) gave eight symptoms of an organisation suffering from bureaucracy – an excess of legitimate power.[14] They are remarkably common in churches – see how you rate:

1. Decisions are invisible: nobody knows where they are taken.
2. Too many tasks are started and not enough finished.
3. Nothing can be done without checking with a host of other people.
4. There is nothing really creative taking place – 'bureaucracies polish but do not invent'.
5. Small problems are seen as major hurdles.
6. There is a tension between the leadership and those in subsidiary organisations.
7. Deadlines become more important than quality.
8. Matters dealt with by the organisation are reactive rather than proactive.

B. Give yourself a hundred marks. Apportion them among the five kinds of power you use, e.g. you may reckon that you use 10 per cent reward power, 5 per cent coercive power etc.

Do the same exercise with your church – either locally or nationally.

Managing for Mission

Our bone structure determines what we look like. Bones may not be visible, but they are an essential part of our being. Like any grouping of people, an organisation needs a skeleton. Even a small group of friends have an invisible structure which determines where they meet, who takes the lead, what they do together, etc.

For centuries people have looked in the Bible to try to piece together the perfect structure for the church. They have not found it, though many would claim otherwise. Some see only bishops, priests and deacons. Others see a mass of Spirit-gifted people swarming around God-inspired elders. Indeed it is not difficult to see a development of organisation during the New Testament period itself, from the first uncertain steps to the more assured and settled pattern shown us in the later epistles. There were probably two factors which shaped the infant church. There was the past in the shape of the Jewish synagogue, and there was the present – the responses demanded by the rapidly evolving situation of the early church growing into a Gentile world. Even if we could find out for certain what the New Testament pattern was, we could never be sure whether it was correct for the present day.

Certain things can be learnt from the mass of material in modern management studies.

About the framework of an organisation

Any structure is **provisional**. Changing circumstances mean that the structure needs to adapt. For example, a strongly hierarchical, authoritarian pattern may be appropriate to a settled environment and a stratified society. But it tends to be inflexible, prone to disputes and uncomfortable to work in. A change in social climate or fresh demands made on the organisation by innovation, increased competition or new marketing techniques will be difficult to adapt to. The faster the change, the more flexibility is required.

For some the church is a bulwark against change, a fixed point in a changing world. Translated into organisational terms this leads to disaster. The result is a dusty, unchangeable, uninteresting museum piece. There is something pathetic about beached whales, out of their element, bewildered and struggling. The out-of-date leader plays tunes which nobody any longer listens to and watches helplessly as people pass by without a glance. Their power has gone.

But not all out-of-date churches appear lethargic. In the first model the past rules, but in the second frenetic activity is uppermost.

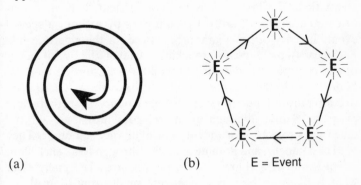

(a)   (b)   E = Event

The first is a church which plans the future by looking in the records in order to copy what was done last year. It replicates rather than creates. It is nearly always in slow decline, because the number of people who are content with merely repeating what has happened before is likely to diminish. If a church service or an event gets its validity from copying the past as faithfully as possible then newcomers are likely to be unimpressed. They have not experienced the tradition which is meaningful to the people in the church. Even for those the tradition can get threadbare. One church 'always' had sausage and mash at every social event. It started as a helpful link with past jollifications, passed through the stage of being a joke and ended as an irritation. Newcomers were merely bemused by this unaltering menu.

A backward-looking church cannot look ahead and so trips over the future. This attitude is often betrayed by the use of the words 'always' and 'never' – 'the Sunday School has always met in the hall at 10.15', 'the harvest festival has always been on the last Sunday of September . . .', 'the Vicar has never done that . . .'. Whenever a church is gearing itself for mission it is essential that the past should not determine the present. It can be a guide and friend, for there is much in past tradition which is helpful, but it should never be elected a dictator.

The crackerjack model is very different (diagram b). It is as energetic as the first is likely to be somnolent. It is the event-orientated church. Hardly a month goes by without a special event. January brings a jamboree service for the elderly, while February is the time for touching some of the social needs of the community, and March heralds an Eastertide mission. Unfortunately these events have no coordination. There is no overall purpose but it gives the *appearance* of activity and progress. Sadly, although great toil goes into these efforts, much goes to waste for they do not build on each other. They tend to compete, and nothing is carried through to a conclusion.

The result is a church with a tired centre. The energies of what is likely to be a comparatively small proportion of the congregation are sucked into the whirligig of endless events. They become worn out with the demands made upon them. A few of the few then opt out, feeling that too much of their life is being asked of them. The rest of the core go on, depleted and disheartened and with a sense of being betrayed by the rest of the congregation. They for their part do not participate, not wishing to be sucked into what seems a pointless series of exercises. However they carry a burden of guilt, which is constantly reinforced by exhortations from the pulpit to be more committed. There is no sense of direction in the cracker-jack church, for the events are not steps in an overall strategy, but merely activity for the sake of doing something. Such a church needs a mission audit when every group and organis-ation can be looked at to see if it is genuinely needed in the light of God's emerging plan for the church.

Sometimes a crackerjack church comes simply from a desire on the part of the leadership to justify their existence. Exhaus-tion becomes the touchstone of holiness. But there is a more common and insidious reason. Developing a strategy means leaving certain things behind. If you are walking westwards you are unable simultaneously to go east. The good is the enemy of the best more frequently in churches than anywhere else. There are so many beneficial things to do – deal with the social issues which surround the elderly, evangelise the young, care for unmarried mothers, pep up the services, reorganise the structure. And so a church sets itself to do them all. But it only has limited resources of people, money and time and cannot tackle all of them. It is all too easy to say, 'We must do something about . . .' and much harder to say, 'If we start doing that, then we shall have to stop doing . . .'. The Japanese do not have a word for 'No', and hence use many circumlo-cutions such as 'Let us think about it'. Many Christian groups follow the same pattern. A strategy means deliberately agreeing *not* to do certain things as well as planning to do things. If this means that for a time the elderly are not top of the agenda, or that certain social issues are not tackled, then this is all right. A factory can only make a certain range of products, and it is likely to find it difficult to change its product range. Russian factories have found it hard to stop making tanks and produce refrigerators. So with a church. The temptation to try to do everything is strong. Keeping clear the vision is one of the main tasks of the leader. There are many interesting sidepaths which look worth exploring but which diverge from the highway that the Lord has set before the church.

Middle management within the church

The distinction between 'line' management and 'knowledge' management is a useful one for the church. The line manager is directly in control of people and production: he or she is normally in some hierarchical relationship with those around them – and, unless they are at the top or bottom of the pile, they are under the direct orders of someone and will have those they can order about. The 'knowledge' managers contribute their particular skills to the company – in personnel management, research and development, and so on. Typically they will be professionals with some qualification in their subject: hence the jibe that the more letters they have after their name the less use they are. They may be freelance, in which case they will charge a fee for their services. Even if directly employed they may be rather outside the main structure of the business – indeed jaundiced line managers have been heard to say that they are parasitic upon it. It is unlikely that the directors of the company have any personal knowledge of what they can offer – and so it is reputed to be easy for R. and D.[1] to conceal their inadequacies and play up their successes.

During the last fifty years there has been great growth in middle-management. Especially this has been true of 'knowledge professionals' – tax accountants, advertising specialists, company lawyers and so on. Commercial life is now more complex and a wider range of expertise is required. More recently, however, the use of information technology has enabled many firms to sweep aside whole layers of line management, so that they feel their jobs are under threat and therefore are even more suspicious of the apparently free spirits who sell their knowledge.

There is often little love lost between the line and the knowledge departments. The line manager may not understand much that the other is saying to him but suspects he is being blinded by science and jargon. The knowledge people are not 'at the sharp end' where production and sales are all-important. They are seen as living in a comfortable ivory tower from which they sally in order to make the job of the line manager more difficult. In the same way knowledge people can see the line managers as lacking in intelligence, and unable to appreciate the fine ideas which they are being offered.[2] There are many weary ministers who would echo the line manager's complaint about other people's enthusiasms, conscious that when all is over the buck stops on their desk.

This distinction has been found to be damaging to a commercial concern. The work of the professionals is not made full use of because of suspicions from line management, and the company suffers. There has been a growing tendency to make sure that different expertise is available at board room level – so most boards will now have a finance director who is an expert in tax avoidance, and sometimes a R. and D. person who can help the board to evaluate the suggestions from that department.

In the church the minister, church committee and the congregation are mainly in line management. Although there may be a wish to break out of the pyramid of hierarchical relationships, they are still there in some form. The minister is still seen by many, however unscriptural this may be, as the M.D. of the company. From time to time the church needs knowledge professionals. A church extension is planned. An architect is called in. Church members may well question the design which emerges, but they are well aware that the architect is the expert who is supposed to know the answers. They may well feel disadvantaged in that they cannot visualise the new building in the way she can and cannot discuss the technical detail with as much background knowledge.

But the church uses more expertise than this form of technical skill. The minister is not only a line manager. He or she has particular skills which come from having studied theology, from past experience or from being educationally a cut above those in the congregation (though it should be noted that a study showed that ministers consistently underestimated the number of graduates in their congregation!). Even if ministers see themselves as having no particular expertise, others take quite a different view.[3]

The minister is not alone. There are others in the congregation who have skills which mean that they are in the position of knowledge professionals rather than line managers. The treasurer may have financial skills, others may bring their skill as a teacher, or an artist or a bureaucrat to the service of God and his church. This is common enough. But there is another group who are particularly valued by the modern church. There are the prophets, the evangelists, the bringers of words of knowledge or of pictures. Churches are taking seriously the injunction of 1 Corinthians 14:26, 'When you come together, each one has a hymn, a lesson, a revelation, a tongue or an interpretation' (RSV). God speaks through different members of the body of Christ.

The same difficulties between line and knowledge management occur in the church as in the commercial world. A church committee, which sees itself as in line management, does not always take kindly to a prophetic word. A congregation is seldom impressed by a flow of incomprehensible theology from the pulpit.

Commerce also finds that the knowledge organisation is much more complex than the line management. The straight hierarchical pattern where the minister or the manager is head of the pyramid is simple, even if ineffective. An organisation where there are many people putting in their own expertise requires far more handling, for often they need coordination and sometimes they will fail to produce what is required. Wisdom can be gained from business practice where it has been found essential that line management is always paramount. The knowledge people should always be servants of the enterprise, not those who make the ultimate decisions. Similarly in the church it is tragic if a prophet usurps leadership and guides the church into his or her own way of thinking, or the evangelist tips the balance of the church by insisting that evangelism is the only thing that a church should do. The task of line management is to make use of these servant ministries without being governed by them.

Businesses have long since found that knowledge workers cannot be treated in such a cavalier fashion as people on the shop floor or in the office. They have to be wooed rather than ordered about. They see themselves as professionals who can move easily from company to company when employment is good. Many deliberately choose to be freelance rather than be tied to a particular firm. Line management's job in controlling them is like leading a symphony orchestra of temperamental musicians. Many in church leadership would have the same feeling. Life may be exhausting but is never dull as the demands of the music group are balanced against the enthusiasms of the evangelist and the cries of the prophet – all of whom may well see their role as the most important in the church.

Peter Drucker draws our attention to a phase in the career of many in the knowledge sector of work: 'knowledge workers . . . are likely to find themselves in a spiritual crisis in their early or mid-forties. Suddenly their work will not satisfy them any more. We need to develop second careers for managerial people when they reach their late forties or so.'[4] Often this is associated with 'plateauing' where those of that age realise that they are most unlikely to be promoted any higher and that no other firm will offer them a better job – they therefore face fifteen or twenty years doing the same work until retirement.[5] Not surprisingly their zest for the job wanes.

Sometimes they are able at this point to branch out on their own as consultants or independent operators, and the record of such moves is good, but obviously it will be those who have been best in their previous work who are able to make the career change successfully. Those in the lower ranks of middle-management are probably 'blocked' – trapped in a situation from which they are not going to be able to move. For ministers the plateauing crisis often occurs when they are in their mid-fifties. They are faced with the question as to whether they should move, knowing that this will probably be to a less challenging position, or to soldier on feeling that by the time they retire everyone will be wanting them to go. Ministers need much help from their ecclesiastical superiors at this point in their lives.

But ministers are not the only ones who have mid-ministry crises. There is a tendency in the church to put people into permanent boxes. It is assumed that the teacher will always teach, the pastor will always pastor, the leader will always lead. I can see nothing in the Bible which says that this must be so. Ministries ought to grow with us, and sometimes new ministries will develop and old ones disappear. I have often seen this in evangelists. When they were young the challenge and the adrenalin-flow it brought were all that they needed as they saw people respond to their God-given ministry. But after twenty years or more they find that it no longer appeals. It is not usually a matter of tiredness, it is rather that God has given them a different ministry – often it is one of teaching and training.[6] Drucker's comment about the need for guidance for people at this mid-life crisis point bears further consideration. So often people need to change and expand their ministries at this stage. They may have been in a certain mould for twenty years or so. They have much experience to pass on to others, but they may well have become stale. God works with our humanity not against it, and he will often put new possibilities and new openings in front of us. It is a difficult stage for anyone, and we shall need help from mature Christians as we are led through this change-over period. A spiritual director is particularly important, for often along with new ministries there needs to develop a new spirituality and pattern of life which accord with the new role. If we are involved in the leadership of a church we should look out for those who need help in this way. A house group leader has become stale, a musician has become type-cast into his or her ministry, an administrator needs to break out of the mould. However, often these people are good at what they are doing and we hesitate to upset what seems to be working well. But if we take no action, their ministry may become self-centred and stale until they become more conscious of their status than their ministry and more proud of their accomplishments than of their Lord.

Increasingly lay people are finding fulfilment in the life of the church which they do not receive outside. There may be a mixture of motives as personal needs merge with ambition for the Kingdom of God. Fortunately he is remarkably tolerant of our uncertain motivations. Women, freed of family responsibilities in their mid-forties, find they have a new challenge in the life of the church, and men who have enough to live on comfortably give themselves to voluntary work as though it was a new career. An increasing number are 'tele-working' – using computers at home which are linked with head office – and are enjoying the ability to apportion their time much as they want.[7] Yet others are unemployed and can find in serving the church something which fills empty lives. This tendency is likely to increase – people who are in the prime of life longing to serve our Lord with all their abilities. Putting before them worthwhile opportunities which are going to stretch them mentally, spiritually and emotionally is part of good leadership, and changing their task sufficiently often to ensure that they do not get stale will be essential.

The influx of such people into the life of many churches is now an accepted fact, and they have much to offer. But those who in their ordinary jobs are efficient and used to taking decisions do not always fit easily into the culture of some churches, where an amateurish bumbling is normal. They may be impatient of meetings which waste time, are badly chaired, or fail to make decisions. Those who come from industries where change is normal, expected and welcome will find that the entrenched resistance to change in some churches is frustrating. The church leadership, especially the minister, may find their enthusiastic contributions a threat, and balk at what they suggest.

In particular they often find the decision making process a mystery. In churches (as in the New Testament) there are many possible ways in which a decision is taken. It may come about by a diktat from the minister or a consensus of the church committee after hours of discussion. It may be the result of pressure from a group within the church or it may come into being no one knows how. It might even be the toss of a coin as in Acts 1. Those who are used to a clear-cut decision making process find this confusing. In particular they find that voluntary organisations like churches tend to be bad at negative decisions: they are better at discovering what ought to be done rather than what ought to be dropped. Yet these difficult decisions are essential.

But these sorts of people need to be used to the full. They are often creative lateral thinkers who can put forward ideas which are truly God-given in order to cut through the fuzziness which often surrounds church matters. Poor or uncertain decisions, hurriedly taken, are not honouring to God. In the 1950s much effort was put into designing faster freight ships so that they could carry more cargo. It seemed the obvious thing to do, but when shipowners stopped to think they realised that ships did not spend most of their time at sea, but in port being loaded and unloaded. Furthermore, the amount of pilfering that took place at the docks was notorious. The answer was not to speed up the ships but to shorten the time spent at the quayside. And so Ro-Ro was born. Lateral thinking brings great benefits, and it is interesting how often the Holy Spirit seems to use this strategy. Christ was a master of it. How often he answered a question by asking another which made people rethink their position . . . 'Let him who is without sin among you throw the first stone . . .'; 'Which is easier to say, "Your sins are forgiven you", or to say "Rise and walk"?'[8]

Middle-management in the church is essential. Without it one person, usually the minister, does all the work. He or she can become like someone digging a hole in the road surrounded by a crowd of onlookers who enjoy watching others work. And the 'life-cycle' of ideas is shortening. Hymns and songs no longer last for generations, liturgies composed twenty years ago already seem dated and new ideas clamour for attention. As the pace of change increases so the importance of the right structure to cope with it becomes more urgent, and these people can be a God-send to fulfil their own ministry and forward the work of the church of Christ.

In some churches thought needs to be given to the marginalised. The position of women is still uncertain. Some quote texts, sometimes with doubtful exegesis, to show that women should have a subordinate role. Others think differently. In many churches, like the Anglican Communion, it is a matter of great debate. Whatever one's personal standpoint the result of the controversy is that women often feel unsure how far their ministry is being accepted. Not surprisingly they wonder if the people they are helping want them to be operating in that position. Research shows that women are more relationship-orientated, and therefore care more about what others feel and think. They will give away their power more easily than men in order to be liked.[9] They are less likely to be prepared to forget the reactions of other people, and so are more sensitive on this issue than men might be in a similar situation.

This means that women working within the church in roles which have been traditionally filled by men need much support, affirmation and reassurance. The leadership of the church will need to realise that many women prefer not to enter confrontation and so will need encouragement to express their views in a meeting.[10]

Those from other countries can also find European or American churches daunting. Besides the obvious problems of communication there is the less obvious language of the body. In Britain to take your jacket off means getting down to work, while in Germany it means you are slacking. Italians regard meetings as of limited value – what happens over lunch beforehand or in the corridor afterwards is far more important. The Irish often use humour to make a point: unfortunately many other countries regard it as trivial. An Arab in conversation with a Britisher will stand closer to him than is expected – so the Britisher retreats, only to be pursued by the Arab.[11] If the person concerned has another colour of skin then the position becomes more than a matter of manners. Racial stereotypes arise which are more serious than images of the Swiss acting like clockwork or the French eating frogs. The church should be a place for all races so that there is neither black nor white but all are one in Christ Jesus. But too often, although now more are welcomed into mainline British churches than used to be the case, there are far too many instances where black people have been denied the leadership positions which they are well capable of fulfilling. Some churches have engaged in positive discrimination, and this may be right to counter the all too visible negative discrimination which is suffered by many black people in their everyday lives.

In his book *New Realities* Peter Drucker asks seven questions of leaders.[12] They are as applicable to church leaders as to managing directors.

1. There is no substitute for 'management by walking around' – not just in the church but in the world outside. This puts oneself in the position of ordinary people – whether in the congregation or outside. How far do we give ourselves time to think through methodically each role within the church, evaluate the people who are fulfilling it, see the strains they are under and decide

what help they need? At the same time we need to look
at people outside the life of the church. Is there anything
in the habits of our church which makes it difficult for
them to hear and respond to the gospel? Is our personal
ministry to them evangelistic? Who is best placed to
communicate with them? A prayerful 'walkabout' can be
immensely significant, either done alone or with a group
of other leaders.

2.   What information do we need to do our job effectively
– and are we getting unnecessary information which
merely overloads the system? Often churches are awash
with the wrong information – much about finance, organisation, charities, and structures and not enough about
people and the local community. (Mission Audit can be
a useful tool in getting this righted, but it has to be
accepted that the exercise itself can give too much information of the wrong kind unless it is well controlled.)

3.   Which tasks do you do which advance the Kingdom –
and which have you merely got used to doing? Cut out
the later: maximise the former.

4.   Communicate. 'Remember, what is obvious to you may
not be obvious to others'. The management expert John
Humble said, 'If you are an accountant, don't talk to
them as though they were also accountants'. He might
have said that ministers should not talk as though everyone else were ministers, Anglicans as though everyone
else were Anglicans, and old stagers as though everyone
else had been in church for all their life.

5.   Check that what you expect to happen has happened. If
not, find out why.

6.   Keep learning. Continuing personal development – in
skills, in spiritual depth and in human maturity – is necessary if we are not to become stale and dull. If one is
working in a technologically based industry it is obvious
that new scientific learning is essential: it is less obvious
but no less necessary for the Christian leader.

7.   Take care of yourself and you will last a long time.[13]

Clearing the Undergrowth

The nature of our work

The Christian leader often works alone, without close supervision, and in an environment which may not have the smooth
efficiency of a managing director's office. One minister told me
that he had not been inside his study for six months: the paper
had eventually defeated him so he closed the door and trans-
ferred to the dining-room table, much to the disgust of his wife.
Whether lay or ordained the leader has to rely largely on self-
management. Nobody is likely to come and suggest better ways
of working and incompetence does not get checked. Even those
lay leaders whose daily work is in an efficient office environment do not always carry this knowledge over to the life of the
church. It is all too common for those who handle tens of
thousands of pounds in their working life to quibble over paper
clips where church finance is concerned.

Without some sense of purpose, planning and perspective
mission does not take place. Often it begins or founders in
the leader's personal discipline. Few churches can evangelise
effectively if the organisation is pulling in different directions,
the administration is chaotic, and the leaders unsure of what
they are seeking to achieve in and through the church.

Many leaders are not sure what their role is. Are they primarily shepherds of the sheep, rescuers of the goats, comforters of
the converted or prophets to the world? This 'role ambiguity'
leads to stress, insecurity and loss of self-confidence. While it
is important for Christian leaders to learn the tricks of time

management studies and mission audit it is more important to know what they are about. At the same time we should not always be searching for our role: it has long since been found in business that there is a vast difference between what managers should be doing, what the management theorists think they are doing and what they really do.

Using our time

Christian ministry is multi-faceted, and it is important to be aware of three elements in our use of time:

> the *amount* of time we work
> the *quality* of the time we work
> the *effectiveness* of our work

It is easiest to discover the amount of time we spend on the various areas of work. A pie chart is a useful corrective to the supposition that we spend all our time in visiting or in prayer or in study. It is possible to keep a careful diary for a couple of weeks and see how much time is spent doing what. Even a careful revue of the last few days will show the relative proportions with reasonable accuracy. (For this exercise it is important to choose a period which is not taken up by something which is untypical – though for some leaders the untypical is typical!)

A representative diagram might be as on p. 126. Possible subjects might be: study, preparation, visiting, conferences/meetings outside locality, networking with others (other church leaders, social workers etc.),[1] prayer (private), worship (public), attendance at church meetings, administration, counselling, evangelistic work, planning/decision making. Around the circumference put a circle with the number of hours involved.

(It is at least as important for the leaders who are not full-time and paid to do this exercise as for those who are. The fact

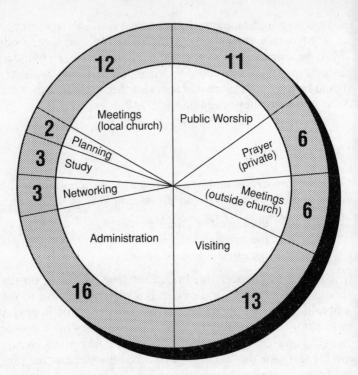

that you have less time to give to direct Christian ministry
within the church means that time is even more precious for
you. Also if you are too busy to do this then you are too busy
– time spent in reflection of this kind is very seldom wasted.)

Almost certainly such a pie chart will show some glaring
inequalities. The most usual realisations which come from this
exercise are:

not much time is spent in private prayer
the amount of study (not direct preparation of sermons, talks
   etc.) is minimal
less time than expected is spent in visiting and counselling

> more time than expected is spent outside the church and its
> immediate locality

The total amount of time which is spent at work is usually considerable. Full-time ministers average fifty-nine hours a week according to one survey – which also showed that superintendents and bishops spent even more.

However it has to be accepted that length of time spent working does not necessarily reflect the *quality* of the time we work. If most of our time is spent at very low levels of efficiency and the rest is spent gazing around, avoiding decisions, passing the time of day with others aimlessly, or reading books carelessly, then the large number of hours is not very praiseworthy.[2] To work forty hours at eighty per cent efficiency achieves far more than sixty hours at thirty per cent. Time is used qualitatively as well as quantitatively. You may find that it is helpful to put round the circumference of your pie chart a further circle estimating the efficiency with which you work at each of the segments and then use a calculator to assess the quality of the time you work. (Do not allow yourself 100 per cent efficiency on anything – it has been shown that total unwavering concentration on something is impossible and probably undesirable – the brain needs to take a brief break from time to time.)

Some find the concept of 'investing time' useful. Each of us has a finite amount of time to use so we should invest it to produce the best result in the same way that a financier will try to invest his money. The Authorised Version has the translation 'redeeming the time' to describe that attitude of seeking to use the present opportunity to the full (Eph. 5:16). While it is possible to become hagridden by the desire for efficiency so that it becomes an end in itself there is also the need for self-examination in this area.

But the number of hours we work divided by the efficiency quotient does not tell the whole story.

To count the number of hours is not too difficult. To estimate the efficiency with which we are working is more subjective and speculative. But there is another question which is in many ways the most important of all and the hardest to answer. We may be working hard and efficiently *at the wrong objective* and therefore completely waste our time. 'Effective management has to be defined in terms of output rather than input, by what a manager achieves rather than by what he does.'[3]

We can see around us people who seem to achieve a great deal with their lives without appearing to work very hard, while others spend ages producing little of lasting worth. 1 Corinthians 3 speaks of our lives producing things of eternal and of merely temporal significance. Because the results of Christian work are often very hard to quantify there is a danger that we look for 'apparent effectiveness' – the outward show of a busy ministry rather than the reality of effectiveness for the Kingdom. To evaluate our *output* is difficult, but important. Almost certainly we shall need the 'faithful friend' who crops up so often in this book – someone who knows us well and who is prepared to be honest with us and our ministry.

By the nature of things, what is urgent is nearly always the thing that gets done rather than that which is important. In particular, mission is usually at the end of the line of priorities: whatever our mind tells us ought to be the case, our diary tells us differently. Mission is capable of being put off to tomorrow, while next Sunday's worship, the meeting to prepare for tonight, the visit which has to be made crowd out the evangelistic work which we are called to engage in. Missionaries talk about the 'Choke Law':

YEAR 1	Evangelism		Admin.
YEAR 2	Evangelism		Admin./Pastoring
YEAR 3	Evangelism	Admin./Pastoring	

In the first year the new missionary has few administrative or pastoral duties and so spends a large proportion of her time evangelising. The second year there are those who are fruit of her work to be pastored and the mission begins to load her with administrative duties. The third year her evangelistic work is down to a fraction of her time . . . One does not need to go overseas to see this happening. Mission is the thing that suffers. It is true in churches and in theological colleges; it is true in the agenda of church meetings and synods, and it is true in budgeting. The essential apostolic work of the church is relegated and its internal workings which seem more immediately urgent take its place. That is why the Decade of Evangelism is so important. It should mean a determined effort to make sure that the outward surge of the gospel is given its rightful place – and it will take all of ten years to make this happen.

The effective leader has to be a 'keeper of the vision' in Josephine Bax's memorable phrase.[4] It is not only a thrilling task. It is also lonely and tiring. To maintain the enthusiasm of others when they seem to have lost their first drive requires the scriptural grace of perseverance on behalf of others. Moses had it in abundance, though it was refreshingly human of him to release the tension in grumbling and anger. While we might object to the title 'great' Henry Kissinger's words apply to any leader, 'The great man understands the essence of a problem, the ordinary man senses only the symptoms . . . the great man has a vision of the future which enables him to place obstacles into perspective; the ordinary leader turns pebbles in the road into boulders'. The Christian leader needs controlled energy – neither a wild enthusiasm which lacks judgement and sweeps others into cul-de-sacs, nor a banal expression of the gospel and of the church which excites no one.[5]

Managing our time

There are numerous books which seek to help us in our use of time. Most of the best ones are not in the religious section of the bookshop. Certain principles stand out, but the main one is that set out by LeBoeuf in *How to Motivate People*: 'Managing time is really a matter of managing your own behaviour'. Most of us find that some ideas are helpful; they are of the 'hints and tips' variety, but none the less useful.

1. If you are feeling out of sorts and unwilling to work then start on a few easy things in order to motivate yourself. But if you are longing to get on with things, start with the tough things so that everything else will seem easier.[6]

2. Cut down interruptions wherever possible. But be realistic – a survey of 160 managers found they worked for half an hour without interruption only once every two days.[7] Some have found it useful to write down the three greatest sources of interruptions and then see what can be done to minimise them.

3. Procrastinators work best when a deadline is looming: they find that work done in good time is not their best because the adrenalin is not flowing. If this is so it is best to acknowledge the fact and make sure that deadlines are set, rather than live in a welter of guilt because jobs are not done until the last minute. This is particularly true of preachers. Probably they were taught in college to prepare their sermons at least a week ahead, but find that Saturday is the time when they really get inspiration. If so, do not feel that it is the sin against the Holy Spirit, but accept that that is how you are. On the other hand you may be the sort of person who is conscientious and meticulous, needs to be well-prepared and finds last minute work unnerving. We need to work within our own personality rather than feel ourselves bound by models produced by people who are not like us. I find more Christian leaders are of the first variety than the second.

4. Time is bound to be wasted if we are unclear what are the goals of the church and of ourselves. Without those

we cannot distinguish what is trivial from what is important. Time spent planning is usually well spent. If a team of Christian leaders is working together they need to spend much time thinking and praying together so that they are 'of one heart and mind'.[8]

5. Time spent in supervision is seldom wasted. The bread-and-butter work of checking that decisions have been properly carried out is routine but essential. Some churches have great ideas but nothing happens because no one person is responsible for progress-chasing. This is particularly important for creative leaders who naturally tend to look to the future rather than the past, for if decisions which have been taken are not carried out there is no springboard for the future. Moreover people will be unable to take seriously any new ideas if nothing has come of what has already been decided.

6. Beware of fatigue. 'Tired doctors make errors, take short cuts, are forgetful and perform at less than their best'.[9] Not only is it inefficient: it can kill. All the caring professions – nurses, doctors, social workers – have abnormally high levels of alcoholism, drug dependence, marriage breakdown and suicide. Like Christian leaders they are often dealing with desperate situations besides which their own domestic crises seem trivial, their work can never be finished, they often live 'over the shop', they carry the burdens of others and worry whether they have made the correct decisions. As one doctor said, 'We are a very vulnerable group. We spend our lives dealing with others and leave no time for ourselves.'

7. Delegate wherever possible, both to share work with others and to develop their skills. The appointment of a secretary or administrator is an important decision for many churches. Most find that it is a decision which should not be taken until the amount of work forces it. Secretaries do not necessarily save time, and they can complicate without forwarding the work of the church.

For some however they are more important than an extra member of the pastoral staff.

8. Identify those people who take up time. A former colleague of mine used to say of some, 'Satan sends them to waste our time'. While not wishing to be so categorical there is no doubt that there are some who need to have their time with the leader rationed. Often they have a particular problem – if so they need to have the relationship 'professionalised' so that they have a definite time with the leader every four or five weeks when they get his or her full attention. This is much healthier than the dependant relationship which grows up when a person is clamouring for attention at every opportunity. When this is decided upon they may initially resent the lessening of time with the leader but it starts the process of weaning so that they become less dependant. There are others who just want to be with the leadership of a church. They may need to be lovingly but firmly asked not to intrude for the danger is that they crowd out more urgent calls – including those of his or her family.

9. Holidays need to be of a decent length to get any real benefit. It takes two or three days to unwind and get the adrenalin out of one's system and another day or two to prepare oneself to return to work. So in a week's holiday there are only a couple of days in the middle in which to relax. Two or three weeks are much more effective in making a real change in one's rhythm of life. Often activists find that a thoroughly tiring holiday walking or hang-gliding or painting is better than lazing around. Sir Nicholas Goodison of the Stock Exchange said, 'Relax, or rather do something different, however busy.'

Administration

Christian leaders are schizophrenic about administration. Many feel it takes them away from 'real work' – which they presumably reckon as leading people to God, preaching, teaching and praying. They inveigh against bureaucracy – whether denominational or local government. They resent time spent at their desk. It may be a good feeling but can have unfortunate consequences, because it can lead to administration being done perfunctorily. This takes much more time in the long run and causes feelings of guilt: it takes far less effort to send out in good time a lesson reading rota than to have to ring round on Saturday evening. It is much quicker to deal with one's mail the day it arrives than to look at it for two weeks before answering.

Peter Rudge describes different Christian leaders in their attitude to administration and pastoral work. 'Some thought of their opposition, others saw the administrative as a necessary preliminary to the pastoral, and a third view was to regard them as intertwined and illuminating each other'. The last, and probably best view, is illustrated by the formidable Victorian Bishop Samuel Wilberforce whom his biographer described as accepting 'the bonds of organisation and administration as an integral part of his pastoral ministry . . . he thought of his committee work and correspondence not as a hindrance to direct pastoral activity, but as its essential concomitant'.[10]

If we still find administration difficult it is best to get down to reminding ourselves that all jobs involve some routine work and uninteresting activities, and the Christian ministry cannot be joy all the way . . .

Workaholism

Either there is something in the Christian ministry which attracts workaholics or the nature of the ministry transforms them.

There are certainly factors which make Christian leaders prone to this disease. The work they do never has an end – they can always pray more, care for more people, study the faith more intensively. Further, most of them work from home: they do not shut the office door behind them or walk through the factory gate. It is easy to confuse the amount of time spent with commitment – so we can gauge our spiritual temperature by how hard we are working. Those of us who are these latter-day Marthas find the Marys who leave us to get on with the work unbearably irritating. Fourthly, they may not have the biblical balance in a servant ministry and see themselves at the disposal of everyone.[11]

Excessive hours worked do not produce much. Contrary to popular mythology, Japanese workers who count it a point of honour to arrive for work before the boss and leave afterwards, actually work at a low standard of efficiency. In this country the eighties' culture produced the 'power breakfast' in order to get meetings out of the way before reaching the office. Could it be that the atmosphere of the eighties came from the top – Margaret Thatcher slept five hours a night, had no relaxations and insisted on a similar pattern of work for those around her. Douglas Stewart, an American industrial psychologist, notes that while such a style of working is one which is usually rewarded rather than frowned upon, 'the short-term gain is a long-term loss' leading to reduced efficiency and stress related diseases. Enthusiasm for work can become addictive, but the research of Professor Carey Cooper[12] shows that after forty-five hours a week work becomes twenty-five per cent less effective and more than sixty hours a week means that the person is putting their health at risk. Someone had a heart attack and had to work reduced hours. It was found that he was achieving eighty per cent of his previous workload in twenty-five hours a week compared with more than fifty hours before his illness.[13]

It has also been found that senior managers inflict their own working patterns on their juniors. This may not be through exhortations to work harder, but through the ethos which the manager generates in the workplace by his or her example. This happens in many churches where a workaholic minister produces a frenetic church. Christian leaders with workaholic tendencies need to beware that they do not surround themselves with those who are similar – the people who volunteer for everything and those who are only too willing to say 'Yes'.

Many organisations have found that one of the few ways of curing a workaholic is to ensure that they go on a sabbatical. Common in academic circles, they are increasingly used in commerce and the life of the church. Those firms which endorse them find that employees come back with renewed energy and enthusiasm. The word is of course biblical: strictly it meant one fallow year off after six years' work (Lev. 25:1–5). Companies usually describe it as 'long leave' or something similar and although some offer a year's unpaid break, most firms and churches regard three months as the maximum and six weeks the minimum. Possibly closest to the sabbaticals which Christian leaders need to take are those enjoyed by journalists. These are seen as 'intellectual refreshment' which enables them to write about and research areas which have interested them and have some marginal relevance to their work. *The Financial Times* calls it 'staff development leave'. Christians leaders I have known have used the time to investigate the healing ministry in Nigeria, travel the length of South America, look at renewal in India, investigate church growth in Korea or go on a preaching tour of New Zealand. Most, however, never leave the country. They spend the time reading theology at a college, or looking at some aspect of the Christian church totally outside their own experience – one looked into ways in which the church could help the probation services and gave a report to the diocese which was acted upon. While some will take it as an extended holiday after many years' work there is no doubt that this does not get the best out of it. There needs to be a time for relaxation but also for purposeful new work.

A word of caution may be in order. Many people going on sabbaticals find that the space means that they lose some of the emotional ties to their church, and the possibility of a move intrudes itself. 'Itchy feet' is a frequent result of a sabbatical.

What is right for those in full-time ministry is right also for others within the church. Church officials need a break from time to time. An organist found that a three-month break gave him an opportunity of visiting other churches, talking to their musicians, going on a course and getting new vision for his work.[14]

Exercise

Employment counsellors produced a test for workaholism by taking a questionnaire based on alcoholism and exchanging the word 'work' for 'drink'. It is a useful check to see if you are a workaholic.

1. Do you feel you cannot control your working behaviour? Do you have difficulty in stopping when you want or do you have bouts of working until you can work no longer?
2. Do you wake up thinking about work? Do you work even harder when you are under stress at home?
3. Have you lost or given up sports and pastimes because of commitment to your work?
4. When you are not working, are you soon irritable, and do you quickly start longing to get back, considering the time off a wasteful intrusion into your 'real' life?
5. Do you find you need to work more and more as you get older, despite your bouts of depression and migraine attacks?

Paul Thorne, a psychologist, would say that your situation is serious but curable if you answered 'Yes' to the first four questions, but if you answered question 5 in the affirmative your health is in serious danger.

Moving into Mission

'Every generation needs a new revolution', said Thomas Jefferson. Mao Tse-tung said the same thing and it led to the Cultural Revolution of the 1960s. Whether the revolution is peaceful or destructive depends on the quality and aims of the leadership. The revolution most churches need is one from facing inwards in self-absorption to facing outwards in mission. And to make the change possible there have to be decisions. A church must take mission seriously. If it has had a mission audit and is left with a list of twelve major recommendations what happens? Sometimes the answer is 'Nothing'. Because it has not taken seriously the disturbance which change involves, the audit is shelved and nothing comes of it: the only result is waste of time and a feeling of frustration which is likely, with reason, to blame the leadership of the church.

The great people of the Bible who took risks were not foolhardy. There are no medals in the Kingdom for seeing faith as a substitute for common sense. They were those who built upon the unchangeable character of God and the rough and ready material of ordinary life. They were basically radical like every successful innovator because they knew they had a dependable God. Even when the way forward meant a complete discontinuity with the past, as when Abraham left Ur, or Paul and Barnabas set out for Asia Minor, it can be seen with hindsight as building upon the strategy of God. It may have been only dimly visible at the time but they had a sense of God's purpose which carried them forward. It has to be admitted though that moving into new territory feels dangerous. Caldwell of Ford

Motors said, 'Exploration, experimentation, enterprise and innovation – all are inherently risky – all are essential to progress'.

Decision-making

The New Testament has a disturbing variety of models of finding out God's will and deciding that something ought to be done. Our Lord communed with his Father and then chose his disciples, taught the crowds and went from Gethsemene to Golgotha. The approach of the early church is more complicated. Acts begins with a future apostle being chosen by the toss of a coin. After Pentecost it seems to have evolved a collective leadership pattern when the apostles decided things together. Once the Church is dispersed through persecution and missionary endeavour then decisions appear to have been made either at the small prayer meeting where it was expected that the Holy Spirit would give the orders or in the more formal setting of a church synod after which it could be said, 'it seemed good to the Holy Spirit and to us'. At the same time there seems little doubt that Paul was the sort of person who followed his own Spirit-guided hunches and did not wait over-long for a committee to make up its mind.

Like it or not mission depends on decisions. Planning a strategy for evangelism means getting certain principles accepted by the church, certain proposals for action put into effect and certain changes in the church made. This can be done by one or two people, or by a church meeting, but usually it falls to a committee to be the decision-making body. Indeed in many churches it is given a legal status which means that some matters must be referred to it. It can be a blessing or a bane. Certainly many Christian leaders are afraid of their committee – either that it will not agree with their own proposals or that it will force through decisions with which they personally do not agree. There are certain principles which are helpful to bear in mind.

1. Decisions have to be made. As Harvey Cox said, 'Not to decide is to decide'. Procrastination solves nothing.

2. It requires a sense of politics from the leaders. What has been described as a 'sense of smell' is difficult to define but all too easy to detect when it is absent. At its best it is the ability to put oneself in other people's shoes and see what the effect of an idea will have on them and how they are likely to react. It may not be difficult to imagine the effect that a proposal to move the war memorial will have on Colonel Blimp but most cases are less easy to elucidate. Some leaders have this political nose to an excessive degree and spend too much time wheeling and dealing. Others are deficient and cause chaos because they have not thought through the implication of what they are proposing: they can look as bewildered as Chicken-licken when the sky falls in.

3. Find out the facts beforehand – and also the opinions. If, for example, the church leadership is trying to introduce new music into the church it is not enough simply to know the price of the new songbook. Knowledge of people's feelings are at least as important. For one the new book may be a symbol of the decadence of modern youth while others think that any change in the church is a change for the better: neither is interested in the merits of the book in question.

4. Collective dreaming should be encouraged. It has been found that something close to wishful thinking has proved a useful preliminary to a decision. Needless to say it has been elevated into a procedure. Known as 'Synectics' it was formulated by Arthur D. Little: this suggests that problems should be tackled by asking questions which begin with 'How can we . . .' which encourages people to focus on the real nature of the problem.

This process takes place far more easily in a relaxed rather than formal atmosphere. Good decisions take time and should not be rushed, and a leader knows which items on an agenda to take briskly and which to linger over.

5.   A decision should be of a suitable size for the organisation. I have heard the church committee of a church with a congregation of a thousand spend half an hour discussing a proposal to paint the church hall kitchen, and a church run by a group of elderly people spend hours discussing how to make contact with the wild youngsters on the street corner. Reverse the situation and it would have been very suitable.

Decisions should come 'not single spies, but in battalions'. A decision should be like a currant in a pudding not an isolated piece of dried fruit. It should fit snugly into the framework of an overall plan. While it is true that often it is only looking backwards that one can see God's will unfold, there needs to be some reason for the decision apart from the need to say 'Yes' or 'No' to a suggestion. Failure to observe this often occurs in mission. Mr Y comes up with an idea for evangelism – possibly it is to concentrate on the young people or take part in a town-wide effort. Unfortunately the decision is not seen as part of a wider whole. It may be that a mission audit has just suggested ways of mission other than those being discussed. It may be that the method of mission proposed has been tried before and found unhelpful. It has to be remembered that *it is too easy to vote for evangelism*. A vote against seems like a vote for sin or at least for lethargy. Some church leaders in Nottingham decided that it would be wrong to put the whole effort of the churches in the city behind the Billy Graham meetings in Birmingham. In part the decision was made on sociological and geographical grounds – East Midlanders have no dealings with those of the West. But the main reason was intuitive: they had a spiritual unease despite the pleading of

those from the Graham organisation and many within the
churches. They received a good deal of criticism, especially
when the campaigns were taking place. When the decision was
made there was apparently no possibility of Graham coming
back to England. In fact the following year he returned to
Sheffield, forty miles away. Nottingham leaders felt that the
time was now right. They threw all their resources into the
campaign and received more referrals from the stadium than
any other place apart from Sheffield itself.

Considerable leadership is required to sideline an idea which
someone has brought forward so enthusiastically. Needless to
say, part of the answer to this zeal is to put forward another
idea in the same area of work which is in accord with the
overall strategy.

Mission also requires **imagination**. First there is the mind-
shift, which has often been alluded to in this book, which means
we stand where non-Christians stand, realise their difficulties
and opportunities and enter into their belief patterns and motivations. Without this hard imaginative work the second kind of
imagination which creates opportunities for evangelisation is
useless. Unfortunately evangelism can become just a matter of
putting on the latest wheeze. Prayer is the way God purifies
our imagination. As we come individually and corporately to
seek 'the mind of Christ' we begin to experience his love for
the world which is deeper than our desire to fill pews and his
creativity which is richer than our contriving. Those who think
evangelistically need time to 'cleanse the thoughts of our
hearts', or it too easily becomes just a re-enactment of the
latest idea we have come across.

Realism is a necessary part of evangelism. Christians tend to
be optimistic people, with justification in the light of the biblical
doctrine of hope. But optimism should not blind us to
unpleasant facts. Business men and women find they have a
tendency to ignore the falling sales figures and the difficult cash
flow situation until the receiver comes through the door: a
Micawberish expectation that something will turn up blinds

them to ugly fact. Indeed it is often on the other side of such unpleasantness that the will of God lies. One church found that the community ignored the glue-sniffers that hung round the local bus station. They saw them as foul-mouthed, dirty and not their business. The church looked calmly at the unpleasant reality, saw the possibility of redemption, contacted them and began to cooperate with the work of God amongst them. In this quiet market town there appeared to be easier people to evangelise, but beyond the harsh fact there shone the light of God and in time many of the youngsters became Christians. It is not surprising that the God who speaks through the cross and resurrection often works in this way.

Accountability

In many churches 'accountability' is the latest buzzword. It means being prepared to explain one's ministry to another who, for these purposes, is in an advisory or even judgemental position. Sometimes this person is a superior in a hierarchy, but at other times he or she may be a friend, a spiritual director or fellow Christian leader. There are certain factors which seem to be common to most forms of accountability.[1]

There are some who fight shy of the whole idea. Christian leaders are accountable to God alone, as Paul himself boasted, 'I care very little if I am judged by you or by any human court: indeed, I do not even judge myself . . . it is the Lord who judges me' (1 Cor. 4:2–4). Others would say that they are accountable only to the local church, and many non-episcopal systems have some procedure of this kind, where leaders are answerable to a presbytery or a congregational meeting. But this kind of close accountability has considerable dangers. If the person concerned is paid by the church it is inevitable that he or she must remain persona grata to at least a majority of the congregation or the elders. This is not always healthy for a prophetic voice or a leader who is trying to move the church in a direction which is God's way and is encountering resistance. This can mean the minister is a prisoner of the church rather than its leader. Though they are not paid by the church, lay leaders are in a similar position and it is too easy when there are clashes of personality or of spiritual perception for the leader to be forced to submit to the power group within the church. Still others see themselves as accountable to their spiritual director or someone of their own way of thinking. But this voluntary choosing of a person may well confuse the 'faithful friend', who is a very important part of a leader's support, with the need to be accountable to someone in authority. This is to deny the catholicity of the church of Christ and tends to be a way of controlling the assessment process in such a way that I only hear what I want to hear.

It has also to be said that assessment has contemporary overtones which cannot be avoided. Some see it as having been used as a political weapon against teachers or doctors, with an underlying desire to cut the cost of education and health care. It has become tied in with attempts to link assessment with performance-related pay. Furthermore assessment at work has sometimes been used as a disciplinary exercise rather than one which seeks to help the employee to develop to the fullest extent. Some Christians have come across assessment in their everyday life and want no part of it within the church.

Yet it has to be asked why people should not be accountable to others in the Church of Christ which has succoured them and guided them in their Christian path, possibly ordained them to ministry and given them a position of responsibility. Whatever Paul said to the Corinthian church about his independence, he twice went up to the 'Vatican' of the early church at Jerusalem to explain his ministry to 'those who seemed to be leaders' (Gal. 2:2). Indeed in his letters he is constantly putting his ministry to the judgement of his readers. He is not afraid of this despite his own independent spirit. Indeed it may be because he was aware of this swashbuckling part of his character that he needed the approval of others of what he was doing.

Many denominational agencies find that younger leaders expect assessment and are disappointed if it is not available or is done inefficiently. Many will have experienced it in a previous area of work, where again it is the younger people who most appreciate assessment. Older men and women were brought up in a different environment and may be more resistant.

Further whether or not formal accountability takes place informal assessment is most certainly occurring. People judge a leader over cups of coffee or round the Sunday lunch table: often the main criterion for the decision is personal like or dislike. It is obvious that such a judgement is unsatisfactory. Frequently those bishops and others pastorally responsible for leaders are reduced to such means of judgement because there is nothing else. Is it possible to devise a method which is more rational and more helpful?

Certainly many at the top of hierarchies think that accountability is a good thing. It will help them with their decisions, and enable them to know more accurately those for whom they are responsible. But those being judged do not always approach the exercise as readily. For them it can seem as though the purpose is not to help them but to aid their superiors. They are nervous about a process which is designed to lay bare the well-springs of their ministry being available to those who have some responsibility for their careers. It is bad enough in an episcopal church, but in one where the leaders are directly responsible to a group within the church the idea of accountability becomes even harder to accept.

For this reason some patterns of assessment ensure that the people involved are not themselves in 'line management', with the right to appoint to future posts. Assessors are brought in who are seen as astute and likely to be welcomed by the leaders concerned. It seems more like a visit to a wise friend than to an assessor. What happens is confidential unless those being assessed give their consent to information being passed on to others.

That senior church leaders wish to delegate this part of their work is not surprising. Managers dislike 'playing God' with those beneath them whom they prefer to treat as professional colleagues.[2]

However it has been found that many leaders actually want to be judged by someone in line management. They value the opportunity to explain what their ministry is about. Most churches have a very wide span of control so that a bishop or superintendent has many to care for. They do not get the day by day contact that is true of most managers and their bosses. It is easy to feel as though nobody knows or cares. Many Christian leaders pine for the question, 'And how are you getting on?', asked by someone who can do something about any deficiencies. They are not content to talk to someone else, however experienced and wise.

But the wide span of control of most of those who fulfil an 'apostolic' role within the church has another disadvantage. Not only does it make them seem remote from the people they are responsible for, it also gives them very limited time with each individual. It is notorious in management that when the span of control is too wide only the noteworthy are noticed – usually those who present problems or those who are outstandingly good. School teachers first get to know the names of the worst and the best in their class. But most local leaders are neither. It is these who feel unnoticed and uncared for and who value good assessment most.

Assessment takes time. Many firms reckon that it takes half a day. Hurried, unthinking assessment by a superior gives the feel of being a nuisance, and it is all too easy for the wrong messages to be read into the process. Yet if a bishop is responsible for 300 clergy it is inevitable that that is likely to happen. Even if he delegates to those on his staff it means a very heavy burden on each of them – and not all the staff may welcome or be good at this delicate work of judging others.

In management circles assessment is normal. Despite the wrong uses to which it has been put on occasion, most people regard it as a routine requirement of the working environment. The usual pattern has three parts.

1. Preparation. Sometimes employees are given a question-naire which asks among other things for their hopes for the future, any home pressures which they wish to speak of and how they see their career advancing. They are also asked about their deficiencies and where they think they need further training. Other firms ask them to write a letter setting out their aspirations and a list of their strengths and weaknesses. It is sometimes found that the freer medium of a letter is more helpful. People who undertake this exercise are often surprisingly frank about their shortcomings – at times they even sell themselves short. Possibly it is an attempt to get the bad news out of the way first.

   Meanwhile the interviewer will be reading the files of those who are being assessed and the questionnaires or letters which have been produced. Nothing gives a worse impression than asking questions which are answered in the material which the interviewee has written – it shows instantly that the interviewer has not read it.

2. The interview. The atmosphere is all-important. Friendly and businesslike seems to be the recommendation given by personnel managers. It should neither seem to be an informal chat nor an interrogation. This means the interviewer should take it seriously, for it is an important occasion for the person being interviewed, but not appear forbidding. It is likely that the employee is ner-vous to some degree and may therefore be defensive before he or she has relaxed. It is wise if the interviewer is sparing of both praise and blame. As one employee of I.C.I. said, 'It is embarrassing being praised and it is embarrassing being criticised'.

3. It is helpful if the interviewer sends those who have been interviewed a resumé of what has been talked about and

especially any decisions about future training, changes in working practices or matters which need to be kept under review. It should not be seen as an opportunity by the interviewer to raise those matters which he or she forgot at the interview or was too embarrassed to ask. It is helpful if a future date – even if many months away – is fixed for a further assessment: this assures the employee that this is part of a continuing process.

This procedure has been developed over many years and it is likely that the Christian Church would be wise to use it as a basis. Some Christian models would wish to include a time for prayer and ministry at the end of the interview, though it has to be remembered that this is not a counselling session, and if there are particular things which surface, the way in which they are to be dealt with should be discussed but not necessarily ministered to on that occasion. Needless to say there should be a time for prayer and quietness during the interview as each person seeks God's purposes.[3]

If the Christian Church cannot give the degree of seriousness to assessment which is normal in the business world then it had better not embark upon it. Yet in the same way that mission audit has become a vital precursor of mission for churches so many leaders are finding that assessment is becoming essential in order that they can find the creative energy and the space for mission. All of us need the assurance that we are doing the right things in the right way, or to have guidance as to how we should improve. It can remove a lot of nervous energy to have someone else who is more experienced than ourselves say that we are doing a good job.

Development training

The assumption that those who have been to college get all the training they need neatly packaged for the remainder of their ministry or that lay leaders have no choice but to pick it up as they go along is rapidly disappearing. The new thinking within the Church, the rapidity of change in society, the Decade of Evangelism have all put a premium upon the need for further training for all in a leadership position.

Certainly as part of any assessment process the possibility of further training should be addressed. Here again the secular world has gone ahead of the church and we would be wise to learn. This is a list of key ideas that one group of management trainers evolved, (only substituting the word 'minister' for 'manager').[4]

(a)   Ministers are responsible for their own learning: it is not sufficient to wait and see if a suitable conference comes along or someone offers a course which sounds interesting. Leaders need to decide for themselves in this vital field of their own self-development. Many denominations have individuals who are expert in this area and can advise.

(b)   People gain insight from the frank views of others. Ministers, like senior managers, seldom hear constructive criticism. They hear grumbles from the dissatisfied but these are easily, and often rightly, brushed aside. The opinion of those we cannot discount is an important part of our self-discovery. Often the most useful views are from those who are doing the same sort of job as ourselves, who can both empathise and yet criticise from a position of knowledge and friendship. Sometimes a group of leaders will form a support group which can be of the greatest help to the members. One group I encountered which was linked with Jesus Caritas had been running for over ten years, with enormous benefit to its members: I was particularly impressed by the rule that people were not allowed to answer 'Fine' when asked how they were.[5]

(c)   Learning is likely to be more effective if it is directly experienced rather than absorbed second-hand through books etc. Christian leaders have often had a tertiary education, and fit easily into the atmosphere of 'unengaged' teaching where they attend lectures, read books and write essays. Educational theory would suggest that it is far better to learn from experience as well as books. To visit another church, set aside time for prayer[6] or work alongside an expert may be much more instructive than reading about that church, or about prayer or about a new area of work.

(d) People need opportunities for personal achievement and creativity. Most jobs stifle creativity by burying it under routine and problem-solving. Training should give space for experimentation, thinking outside one's own orbit, making new discoveries. Gallwey saw two aspects of personality. The first was Self One which judged, criticised and was preoccupied with success. Self Two on the other hand was intuitive and more in rhythm with life. The flights of fancy of Self Two tend to be crushed too soon by Self One and so 'personal creativity can be enhanced by finding ways of quieting the parts of oneself which promote tension'.[7] In those training courses I have been involved with it is obvious that the two or three day conference is not sufficient to give participants time to switch off Self One sufficiently to allow Self Two to begin to blossom. Courses of only a few days are of very limited value and it may be that one or two continuous weeks' development training each year should be regarded as necessary.

(e) More choices exist than people generally realise. Training should give the opportunity for lateral thinking – to realise that there is nearly always more than one solution to every problem, and more than one pathway up each mountain of vision.

(f) Emotions and feelings are an important part of an individual and it is dangerous if we ignore them. Some would see this as a particularly British oversight for in the affairs of state as well as in the Church emotions are not supposed to exist. Philip Greenslade says, 'For a long time we took our leaders out of the deep freeze and wondered why our Christianity was so uninspiring'.[8] The reason that some leaders prefer the academic model is that it is less personally threatening. The apprentice model based upon direct experience requires engagement by the whole person. The master craftsman shows you how to carve the wood, and then says, 'You have a go' – and then criticises as you do it. Moreover the space which training provides means that it can be a time for release and healing of the emotions as well as input for the mind. There should be little training of more than a day or two which does not give an opportunity for ministry.

(g) Relationships with others can often be deepened beyond one's expectations. This is particularly true of those we work with regularly. Taking the same training course or experiencing the same new work of God can do much to move relationships with fellow-leaders and colleagues off a merely 'technological' level – concerned with the work you do together rather than a real meeting of person with person. It is for this reason that firms send groups of employees on courses on mountain climbing or windsurfing, for it is in positions of some stress and even danger that friendships and mutual dependency grow, as the armed forces have known for generations.

(h) It is vital to experience one's own individuality. Training gives an opportunity to be oneself, especially if it takes place away from one's normal environment. To make relationships with a different set of people, see how one reacts to new ideas and think through one's own ministry can give back to some people a sense of themselves. The disciples experienced it when they

were pulled from their routine jobs by Christ. Before
that event they had a predictable life to look forward
to, living in the same neighbourhood, meeting the same
people, taking their expected place in the community.
The call of Christ opened new possibilities so that one
fisherman came to lead the early church and another
wrote a poetry which still makes us tremble with the
beauty of it.[9]

There are few Christians who could not see the value of such
criteria. Indeed if you have had a recent experience of learning
it is good to put it alongside them and see how far they were
achieved. Whether it was formal training such as a conference
or a visit to another church or the reading of a book it is a
useful check-list.

Woodcock and Francis would want to say that it is also
important to identify the blocks to learning. If these are more
powerful than the desire to learn then it is likely the opportunity
will be wasted. They identify:

  (i)   personal laziness. This is often experienced as what
        the medievals called accidie – the sin of retreating into
        passivity, and bumbling along waiting for 'something
        to turn up'.

 (ii)   difficulty in overcoming tradition enough to ask, 'Why
        do we do that?'

(iii)   excessive tension. Often this is seen as an overconsci-
        entiousness which demands perfection in all things and
        is personally threatened by rough edges. It is helpful
        to remember that almost every mechanical contrivance
        has a 'working tolerance' – plus/minus 2 mm for
        example. Fortunately few areas of ministry require
        exactitude and most experience is built upon mistakes/
        The explorer Sir Vivian Fuchs said, 'Good judgement
        is the outcome of experience . . . and experience is
        the outcome of bad judgement'.

 (iv)   an unwillingness to change. This can be hidden under

a martyr complex: I have heard too many leaders claim that 'I work in the hardest church in the most difficult area in the country' to believe them entirely. They may come to be of the opinion that they have no need of learning or personal growth. Judson Cornwall wrote of those whose charisma outstripped their character, 'pride in their successes, attitudes of superiority over other ministers, resentment towards people for the pressures they exerted on them and inflated self-evaluation of their own personal worth took its toll'.[10]

(v)   insufficient opportunity – lack of information about training possibilities, shortage of money to pay for them, a diary which is too busy for training.

(vi)   over-seriousness. Sir Roy Sission of Smith Industries has said that the requirements for management are: 'The Three Hs' – Humanity . . . Humility . . . Humour. The last is an important tool of learning. We learn best when we have a playful attitude and enter into the excitement of new ideas. The opposite is an attitude of aloof detachment. We gain most when we throw ourselves into something, while keeping our Self One alive so that we do not climb uncritically on a bandwagon.

(vii)   a poor methodology in which the person being trained is unable to put the new thinking into practice. A particularly important tension comes between the practical urge to get something done and the pastoral fear of upsetting people. As new ideas are introduced, at the back of the leader's mind is the thought, 'Mr Y would never stand for that'. It prevents new ideas from being thought about, let alone adopted. This tension is particularly common in Christian leaders and has to be tackled if new thinking is to be absorbed. There are some leaders who are much troubled by the perception that others have of them. Those who manage stress well are not excessively disturbed if other people disapprove of them.

Mission requires efficiency from the leader. This in turn demands constant learning in personal and professional skills or the wish to evangelise and lead the church in mission is lost in ineffectiveness or personal inadequacies. Christ led his disciples on the same path. By being with him and seeing how he worked they learnt the skills of ministry and his 'spiritual direction' of each of them, seen most clearly in the case of Peter, led them to self-understanding and reliance upon him.

The Spirituality of Evangelism

Evangelism is a very busy word. It suggests activity – missions and campaigns, words spoken and printed, people being persuaded. It is energetic. The word evokes images of crowds and bustle. It speaks of confident assertion and the proclamation of truth, even of brashness and noisiness.

Spirituality is a quiet word. It suggests silence and quiet retreat, prayer and meditation. Spirituality is our aloneness in the presence of God. Here the flavour is one of exploration and a search for the truth.

Neither evangelism nor spirituality are words which are easily defined. Yet Christian evangelism must have a spiritual base if it is to have integrity. Otherwise it degenerates into mindless activism without reference to God and without power. Similarly spirituality without thought of mission becomes selfish. The two elements must intermingle and the Christian leader intent on leading a church in mission will want to ensure that there is a spiritual evangelism and a missionary spirituality within the church.

Spirituality cannot be a means to an end. It is true that much prayer can give people the psychological boost they need to go out evangelising but this is a by-product. Prayer is not a motivation for doing something else – it must stand in its own right at the heart of evangelism.

A much more fundamental difference is the common Western supposition that evangelism has to do with 'them' – that it is essentially looking outwards towards people and structures. Spirituality however has to do with 'me'; it is the journey inwards to the ground of my being. It is a Western outlook which tends to see spirituality in such quiet and even pietistic terms. The liberation theologians from South America see spirituality in much more robust terms in 'breaking down strongholds' of oppression. Feminist theologians speak of a women's spirituality which is much more active than thinking beautiful thoughts with folded hands.

There is a considerable danger in a 'me' centred spirituality. It can become at worst psychological self-delusion in which prayer is seen as me communing with myself. Meditation may or may not be good for us physically, mentally or spiritually because we need to have a time when we turn from our business. But that is not its real purpose which is to bring us into the presence of the God whom we can adore. At best this spirituality can be seen as the soul in communion with God, thanking him for what he has done for me, praying for my concerns and being personally healed and refreshed. But if this is all that spirituality is then there is something seriously wrong, for it has become a thoroughly selfish activity. Even prayer can become self-indulgent. Once I ministered to a woman who had fallen into the hands of spiritualists. She was instructed to imagine that she was walking in a cool white garden with her 'guide' who would talk to her and show her beautiful things. Her real life was humdrum and, not surprisingly, she began to find that 'walking in the garden' was a great deal more exciting than going to work or cleaning the house. In the end she admitted to spending up to ten hours a day in this exercise. The garden had become for her the real world: the imaginary had become concrete and actuality no more than a haze around the imaginary. If Christian prayer ever becomes such an escape into ourselves and our concerns, then there is danger.

Generalisations can be facile, but the thought patterns of the Western world in the 1960s encouraged an era when personal happiness, self-fulfilment and development of the personality became paramount. Rights become more important than responsibilities, and self-expression was the highest good. A plethora of courses to enable people to develop and become themselves was started. It was called the 'me' generation. Some areas of the church tended to take over these ways of thinking uncritically, failing to recognise that they were all basically selfish and unchristian. Some forms of meditation, stress upon 'healing of the self', and the claim that the Christian life was 'good for you' tended to flow with the world, rather than examine its presuppositions. At its most obvious it produced 'prosperity teaching' which sees Christian commitment as a worthwhile investment which every financial adviser should recommend.

At the same time the technological advances of the world during the same thirty years have given evangelism tools which it did not dream of. Television, satellite communications, improvement in printing gave the possibility of a much greater spread of certain people's views – if they had the money to command. On the other hand advances in educational methods, and, more sinisterly, an understanding of how it was possible to manipulate people into acceptance of a view which they did not previously hold gave evangelists techniques which needed but did not always receive ethical examination before they were accepted.[1]

All this meant that evangelism was seen more and more as something which people did to others, rather than as a relational interchange. Seen at its most obvious in the 'tele-evangelists', evangelism became non-personal – though the latter used a folksy studio set to emphasise that it was truly human.[2]

The interiorisation of spirituality and the almost mechanistic view of some evangelism meant that there was a widening divergence between the two with little expectation of common ground. This needs to be corrected, for as evangelism without prayer is dead, so spirituality without the urge to look out in concern for the world becomes over-intense and self-serving.

It is in the reason for evangelism that the rapprochement can be seen. 'God so loved the world that he gave his only-begotten . . .'. The apostolic ministry of the church mirrors the apostolic ministry of God himself. We are sent to love because God in his love has first sent his Son.

Indeed without agape *nothing* is of value. 1 Corinthians 13:1–3 says that without love the charismatic gifts of tongues, prophecy and martyrdom are totally useless. It is not only those three gifts for which love is essential. They apply to everything which the Christian church does. If there is no love there is nothing. 'At eventide they will examine thee on love' as St John of the Cross said. It is the necessary underpinning of both evangelism and spirituality.[3]

To love someone is to be concerned for their full welfare. If we are parents we want our children to be full human beings – not only to know their Bibles and pray every day but to be emotionally secure, reaching their full potential, having rich relationships. In the same way we should want our neighbour to be fully human. Prayer which comes from love does not just pray 'that they may be converted' – it prays that they may be full human beings. And the most important ingredient of reaching their full humanity is that they are in a relationship of trust with our Creator.

The same is true of groups. Christ had compassion for the crowd who were 'like sheep without a shepherd'. He longed for their good. This yearning was at the root of both his prayer and of his evangelism. We need the same concern for the crowds who surround us in cities or for those whose mute faces stare at us from the TV screen after some disaster. But it is overwhelming – there are too many people, too much disaster, too many demands upon our pity that we eventually shut off in self-protection. We suffer from 'care fatigue'. Christ loved and loves. We must remain vulnerable. The words of Mother Teresa may help. When taken to an unfamiliar Indian city and shown an area of destitution, her guide said despairingly, 'What can we do to help so many thousands?' She said, 'You work by addition: I work by subtraction'. She saw the crowds as a collection of individuals – if she brought only one into a fuller life she had helped the situation. Her friend saw only the mass and was crushed.

To lead a church into an evangelistic spirituality makes deep demands upon the spiritual resources of the leader, and there are two areas where there is particular need of sustenance. The first is the spirituality of pain, for to deal with the real world rather than the make-believe world of the church is to encounter pain. The other is to have an understanding of joy and hope, otherwise the pain overwhelms and we never move from cross to resurrection.

The spirituality of pain

Christian leaders must show the way of love, and help others to follow it. It is easy to allow less worthy motives for evangelism to come to the fore – to build up our church, to make our mark on the neighbourhood, even to fulfil my ministry. 'Seek first the Kingdom of God . . . and all these other things [church growth, community involvement, personal fulfilment] will be added to you'. The pain of love can be intense. Modern counsellors are taught to empathise – to sit alongside and understand the pain of others without being themselves sucked into the vortex. Christ went further. He sympathised. He entered the pain of others and suffered with them. He wept at the tomb of Lazarus, his whole being ached as he saw the cortège come out of the city of Nain, and on the cross the sin and suffering of the world consumed him. But, in bleaker moments some leaders say, 'It was all right for him – how can I sympathise and yet protect myself from being overcome?' Leaders need a spirituality of pain.

Some personalities surround an experience of pain in the way an oyster marginalises a grain of sand. The pain is put on one side and they carry on with life. Others are haunted by the experience, think of what they might have done further to improve matters, and wake up in the night worrying. Yet others develop a carapace of seeming indifference: those ministers whom Wilkerson described as 'having become tough in the service of the gospel'.[4] This problem is faced by all the caring professions, and nurses and social workers have a more harrowing time than most Christian leaders: any lessons which are learnt will be gratefully received by them.

If Christ taught us to be vulnerable, he also taught us how to bear the pain of it. One element was the constant prayer to the Father – he passed to his Father both the pain of the other and the answering pressure upon himself. As he was being pinned to the cross he handed over to his Father the sin of his executioners: 'Father forgive them . . .'. Christian leaders must do the same if they are not to become hard-boiled or indifferent.

The second part of the spirituality of pain is to ensure that it is shared. But it must be shared only with appropriate people. We need to take care as to what is right to pass on to our marriage partner. The divorce rate in all the caring professions is higher than average, and that amongst ministers is about average. Part of the joy of marriage is sharing the burdens. But to inflict the pain of others excessively on to one's partner means he or she is being asked to bear these burdens as well as their own. Further, if their own concerns seem petty and unworthy it may be difficult to give them much sympathy. If a leader comes home after being involved with a tragedy of death and bereavement it is hard to summon up much concern over a blocked pipe in the washing machine.

Some will turn to their bishop or superintendent. Most people in such positions of authority invite such freedom of expression. Bishops see themselves as fathers in God, available pastorally to all their clergy. In practice it does not work smoothly. The one in authority is often too busy to give much time and they may give instant answers rather than be able to tease out the ramifications of the situation. There is another inhibiting factor. Those who are in line management in a hierarchical structure have more than pastoral responsibilities for those under them. They make decisions about the future. They wield temporal as well as spiritual power. This means that there are two agendas operating. One is the problem which has brought them together, but underneath there are other questions, 'If this means that she can't handle stress, I ought to rethink that post I was considering suggesting', 'I need to show myself in the best possible light . . .' Generally it is best for people to seek other resources of help unless authority has to be told because of the nature of the problem.

The best people to share pain with are those who themselves know the pressures of ministry. They should not themselves be emotionally involved. They should have enough insight into oneself and the situation to be able to give good counsel. These three requirements are most likely to be met by colleagues or groups where you can be truly open, or by spiritual directors. But this is not always easy. The Church seldom provides adequate sounding boards, though gatherings of ministers like clergy chapters and fraternals are supposed to give that sort of mutual support. But they are entirely clerical – for the lay leader there are few resources. Too many give up at this point: 'We have nobody to turn to'. If this is true then it must be the responsibility of the leader as a matter of priority to find such people to help. I have seldom found a Christian leader refuse to give such support to another – indeed most regard it as a privilege to do so. We should be braver about approaching our brothers and sisters and asking for help. Even in extreme situations which may demand much time most will respond favourably, for as one such said to me, 'To rescue the ministry of another is the most important thing I can do'.

But there was more to Christ's spirituality of pain than prayer and the sharing of anguish with his Father. He showed emotion. A minister told me that he felt a failure: a few weeks before he had gone to a home where a boy of sixteen had just killed himself sniffing glue. He was an only child and his father had disappeared long ago: the mother was left alone. He said, 'I could not pray with her, I could not read a verse from the

Bible: all I could do was put my arms around her and weep with her: I felt totally useless'. It did not require much insight to recall Romans 12:15 which commands us to 'weep with those who weep',[5] nor was I surprised when he said, 'She has been coming to church every Sunday since the funeral – I don't know why'. Christ expressed his real self to those around him – people are drawn to an individual either because they are famous, or because they manipulate people, or because they have warmth and humanity. In the Temptation Christ refused both the hero-worship of the crowd and the power of manipulation – it was to his personality that they were drawn. We hear of him weeping, being filled with both compassion and anger, being racked with anguish and being transported with joy.

Some Christian leaders feel that they must keep an impassive face to the world, coolly professional, giving themselves to no one. The tradition of the church has not always been helpful – 'do not make friends in the congregation' is advice still given to young ministers; 'do not let your personality intrude in your conduct of worship' is still an ideal set by some teachers. They are dangerous half-truths. The gathering of a coterie of friends around any leader is foolish, just as worship leaders who point to themselves rather than to God are abusing their position. Far more serious though is the underlying supposition that leaders should hold themselves back from the congregation. I once talked with a bishop about ministers who were found to have sinned in a way which was serious and yet still enabled them to stay in their pastorate. How were they regarded by their church? We both remarked that often the church grew in numbers and the relationship between the minister and most of the congregation improved. After such an episode the minister is now seen as fully human, fallible like themselves and therefore more approachable. Only a few Mrs Grundys refuse to extend forgiveness. This is a method of church growth which is not mentioned in the books, and I am not recommending it, but underneath is an important truth: the congregation need to know that they are led by a real human being, a sinner as

well as a saint. Past leaders are often remembered affection-
ately more for their foibles and failings rather than their sanctity
and their teaching. It may be humbling to remember that that
is how we shall be seen in years to come.

Just as Christ expressed his feelings at Nain, at Gethsemene
and at Bethany to those around so should the Christian minister. We should be prepared to share them not just with God
as Father but with our family in Christ. The surge of real
concern and support is wonderfully uplifting. Christ did not
only support the disciples – they supported him.

But this is not always possible. Some matters are too confidential, some are too private and some are too personal. Some
can be shared with a few – many leaders have their equivalent
of Peter, James and John within the congregation with whom
they can be more open, and who will not abuse the trust
being put in them. Some matters can be shared outside the
congregation with the sort of support discussed above. But
some have to be kept to oneself. This is the burden of leadership so graphically described by St Paul in 2 Corinthians 6:6–7,
'We recommend ourselves by innocent behaviour and grasp of
truth, by patience and kindness, by gifts of the Holy Spirit, by
unaffected love, by declaring the truth, by the power of God',
or as Harry Truman put it, 'The buck stops here'.

The spirituality of joy

Some ministers wear their calling like a hair shirt. Others see
it as a fine suit tailored in heaven. To see only the pain is neither
sensible nor true and some forms of spirituality encourage
self-abnegation in ways which are not healthy. The biblical
injunction to 'deny yourself' does not mean leaving behind all
that is pleasant and beautiful and satisfying. You deny yourself
in order to 'follow Christ'. It is the beginning of discipleship,
but Christ does not always lead along rough paths. As Samuel
Rutherford said, 'I am taught in this ill weather . . . to put

Him between me and the storm: and (I thank God) I walk on the sunny side of the brae'.[6]

Paul spoke of much pain, but also of much joy in his ministry – and his greatest joy were those he ministered to: 'my dear friends, whom I love and long for, my joy and my crown'.[7] Those who do not rejoice in their congregation are all too liable to become cynical and depressed. I find it exhilarating to hear a leader enthuse about members of the church. As an outsider I may find them unimpressive, but she looks with the eye of love and speaks about someone who has just found the reality of God, another whose life has been transformed, a mentally handicapped man who has been accepted, the widow who has found purpose in the life of Christ.

Secondly, the Christian life is in essence optimistic. It is the most realistic of religions. The incarnation speaks of accepting the degradation of life and the depravity of which humanity is capable. But, knowing this, it speaks of redemption and hope. One leader I was with was facing a horrendous problem in their church – people were at each other's throats, the spiritual life seemed dry and leading worship was like wading through treacle. But this new minister was strong in faith. He said, 'God has put me here in charge of this, and, provided I use the right methods it will be all right'. I asked him what it meant to 'use the right methods'. He replied that it meant renouncing what Paul called 'practising cunning' – politicking in the church committee, forming cliques, going behind people's backs. It meant relying on prayer and openness and meekness of spirit. It was less than a year when I returned. The transformation was remarkable. Not every problem had been solved, but there was a new sense of cooperation rather than competition in the church, there were new people being added to the church each week, the old sores were beginning to heal, and, above all, there was a sense of worship and joy about the place. It had been leadership of a very high order, though my friend would probably not have recognised it as such.

Part of this optimism is the way in which the leader looks at the congregation. I can remember looking down the church at a Sunday service and seeing nothing but problems . . . Mrs Jones was about to create about the new music, Mr Smith was terminally ill, I suspected that Jack was having an affair with Jill. This was not the way of Christ, who looked at the disciples, saw them in all their unpleasant reality, loved them and by doing so changed them. Paul speaks of his love for the Corinthian church and his hope for their future, despite their quarrels, their immorality and their doctrinal confusion. Perhaps the element in the trinity of 'faith, hope and charity' that leaders are most tempted to forget is 'hope'.

Thirdly there is the joy in the gospel. Preaching is not preaching unless it is also testimony. These truths which I proclaim I have myself rejoiced in. Nowhere is this more important than in a church engaged in mission. The basics of the gospel – the incarnation to save us from our plight, the glory covered cross, the new freedom prefigured by the resurrection, the exhilaration of the Spirit – need to come time and again to our own lives so that we can share them with integrity.

I have spent so long on the spirituality of the leader because that is the emphasis of the Bible. Congregations reflect the life of the leadership. Ministers tend to produce clones. It is unnerving that an older leader attracts older people, a scholar attracts the intelligentsia. There may be many exceptions to this, but there are few to the more basic truth that a spiritually bankrupt leadership will produce a church which is spiritually slovenly where worship is dull and the prayer life unadventurous. Ultimately it will probably be materially bankrupt for few will attend.

The pastoral epistles were written by a leader to a leader. They give advice on how to run a church. But they are also full of exhortations to personal holiness of life and the need to 'stir into flame the gift from God which is yours through the laying on of hands'.[8]

Stephen Cox from an inner city church in North London

wrote of the battle of prayer which he experienced as he started groups for those enquiring about the faith: 'Fruit only began to come in a substantial way during the year when I committed myself to lengthy, sustained and often gruelling prayer for each member, individually by name on a daily basis . . . it is a time-consuming process. It means a commitment on the part of the leaders of the group, and preferably of many more in the church, to see prayer as a really major part of their task . . . I find it the toughest, most tiring part of the whole process'.[9]

A meditation for Christian leaders from 1 Corinthians 13

'Love' which Paul uses in the first three verses is a very big word and *agape* can become a 'glory' word.[10] Impressive in sound but signifying nothing. In vv. 4–7 he draws out the implications of *agape* in practical terms.

Are we *patient* with people – not just putting up with them but staying with them in their highs and lows?

Is our leadership *kind*, or does it ride roughshod over those who get in our way?

Envy has at its root the comparing of ourselves with another. It is impossible to lead in 'collaborative ministry' unless we are free of it for as soon as someone becomes more capable than ourselves in some field of ministry we reject them rather than rejoicing in their God-given abilities.

To *boast* is to become tedious. The very rare Greek word may suggest 'wind-bag' – someone puffed up by their own self-importance. For a minister it is to lose the respect of their congregation (it is usually a male sin). There is a laughable side to this – the petty pompinjay strutting pretentiously on his little stage.

To be *conceited* is to be guilty of the fault which leads to boasting. It indicates a lack of integrity in ministry. It shows we do not know ourselves, and find it difficult to judge how others see us.

We need to realise the true meaning of the word usually translated *rude*. *Aschemoneo* means 'to act dishonourably' – not according to the schema, the proper pattern of things. Leaders are people on show, expected to fulfil a role which can be suffocating. It is very human to step out of role and delve in the dirt.

We are all *selfish* . . . I-centredness has to be consciously rejected and again and again we have determinedly to put others first.

To be *quick to take offence* brings to mind those leaders who have a short fuse. They stand on their dignity, interpret criticism of what they propound as being a personal attack, are offended if their honorific titles and academic qualifications are not mentioned. Overbearing Christian leaders are not an attractive sight. It suggests touchy characters who are unsure of themselves, needing always to bolster their self-image by pouncing on any real or imaginary slight.

If a leader harbours resentment for what was done to him or her long ago and keeps a *score of wrongs* it means they are likely not to have been able to accept for themselves the glory of the gospel. God forgives and forgets. This may sound trite but a failure to do this leads to a ministry which is an exercise in 'damage limitation' where leaders become paranoid in the supposition that everyone is trying to harm them. The world becomes hostile, unwelcoming. Therefore, they argue, it is safer to trust no one, allow nobody close to you, suspect the motives of anyone who appears friendly.

One would think that to take *pleasure in the sins of others* is hardly something which most Christians would aspire to. Surely as those who uphold righteousness they should get no enjoyment in sin. Yet it is all too common in covert forms. The Greek verb is used of keeping financial accounts and suggests keeping a careful record. Many are secretly pleased to hear of the transgressions of leaders in other churches, and find their own status enhanced when they hear of trouble elsewhere.

This searching paragraph ends more positively. To *delight in the truth* is the right attitude for the Christian. Truth found where it is not expected is particularly important – it may be from those who theologically you disagree with, or from those of other faiths or none. The Holy Spirit guides into truth and away from fantasy-land: a mirage which is forever shrouded or always sunlit according to personality and circumstance.

Epilogue

The leader walks along a narrow ridge. On the one side lie many beckoning byways. One entices into the jungle of counselling and the church fails to be led adequately. Another beguiles by the politics of the community and the church is left rudderless. Another dances down the exciting road of pure evangelism leaving a church exhausted and unpastored.

On the other side of the ridge lies the tunnel which narrows the vision until it can concentrate only on the church and its inner life. Parochialism closes in until the church becomes the world and the world shrinks to a surrounding shadow.

The argument of Romans 12 is that each person with a ministry should concentrate on his or her ministry, '. . . if you are a leader, lead with enthusiasm'. It will not be the only thing that they do but that is the direction in which they should guide their life. The Anglican Ordinal suggests the same:

> Serve them with joy, build them up in faith, and do all in your power to bring them to loving obedience to Christ.

The job of the leader is to lead. It requires skill and application, and the ability to both receive and give criticism. It demands a commitment to God, to the people of God and to the community. The basis can only be love honed in the demands and pleasures of ministry.

I hope this book has helped to show that there are skills to be learnt and lessons to be learnt, but not I trust at the cost of our humanity. The person of Jesus did his Father's work – but among people and their concerns, not always in the synagogue and the religious place. No one more truly human but no one more truly dedicated.

It is a privilege to lead the church. To lead it in mission is glorious indeed as it begins to act out its apostolic role.

It is not surprising that the Ordinal, having spelt out the privileges and pressures of ministry, concludes:

> Because you cannot bear the weight of this ministry in your own strength but only by the grace and power of God, pray earnestly for his Holy Spirit. Pray that he will each day enlarge and enlighten your understanding of the Scriptures so that you may grow stronger and more mature in your ministry, as you fashion your life and the lives of your people on the Word of God.

Notes

Chapter 1. Leadership in the Decade

1. They often used to be called House Churches, but that name is hardly satisfactory for churches which meet in the largest building in town.
2. *The Age of Unreason* (1988).
3. Professor of Mission at Fuller Theological Seminary, California.
4. Max Boisot, *Information and Organizations* (1987).
5. It may seem strange to encounter apparently ecclesiastical words like 'mission' in the business world but it is common modern usage as is the term 'mission audit' which is also widely used as a description of the process which leads to the 'mission statement'. Both phrases apparently started in the Church: I believe the first use of 'mission audit' is in *To a Rebellious House* (1981).
6. Bill Quirke, Managing Director, in *People in Business*.
7. The exception to this need for consultation is in a crisis situation. When he took over the demoralised Eighth Army in 1942 Montgomery immediately called his staff together and told them what he intended to achieve and the changes which were therefore necessary. It is not recommended for many pastoral situations.
8. Peter Drucker, *Management* (1977). In this book management and leadership are used interchangeably as in most modern books. No one has drawn any meaningful distinction between the two, and modern management theory draws no distinction between them. This book uses the word leader for those in authority within the Church since that is the commonly used term, but no weight should be given to the distinction: cf. *Understanding Leadership*, pp. 6, 7. A few make a distinction: e.g. 'Managers do right things. Leaders do things right' (Warren Bennis), but it does not stand up to close examination. Godfrey Golzen and Andrew Garner in *Smart Moves* (1990) equivocate by talking about 'managerial leaders'!
9. *The Human Side of Enterprise*.
10. *Gods of Management* (1985).
11. Janet Richardson of the Leadership Trust.
12. The 'Changing Church Course' held in Birmingham each year. Further details from: 5 The Green, Willow Park, Wrenthorpe, Wakefield WP2 0JP.

13. Golzen and Garner, *Smart Moves* (1990).
14. An Alban Institute paper by Rouhage, 'Sizing up a congregation for new member ministry' identified the 'gatekeepers' who were normally present in a small church upon whose approval all newcomers, including the minister depended. In one village where I served these were popularly known as the 'The Royal Family'.
15. Charles Hampden-Turner, *Corporate Culture for Competitive Edge* (1989).
16. Within the organisation there will be certain 'culture carriers' – individuals who set the tone of the group or organisation. It may be the company chairman or the minister. It is often a person who by the force of their personality determines how others think and behave. It does not have to be people near the top of an organisation: the unhelpful impact of the 'canteen culture' in the police force has been often documented.
17. *Information and Organisations* (1987).
18. P. F. Drucker, *Innovation and Entrepreneurship* (1985).
19. P. F. Drucker, *Management*.
20. In this I follow Professor Charles Handy, *Gods of Management*.

Chapter 2. Look at all the People

1. I have used the traditional term of 'spiritual director' to describe any person who is seeking to help another to grow into Christ – whether their 'client' is a Christian or not. Chapter 3 sets this out more fully.
2. Kroeber and Kluckhohn, *Culture: a Critical Review of Concepts and Definitions* (1952).
3. I am far from happy with this umbrella phrase, which is extremely inexact, but it is often taken as those areas where the results of the Enlightenment are most obvious. But virtually everyone in the world is under that influence to a greater or lesser degree. However I have used it because it is generally understood.
4. There are those that would argue that this comparative indifference is due to the poisons of the individualism of the Enlightenment having corrupted the Church. I do not think so: it is part of the gospel that we are responsible before God for our own response to its teaching.
5. This is also reflected in the famous statement of Acts 1:8: '. . . to Jerusalem, Samaria and unto the ends of the world'. Here Samaria can be taken as the 'half-Jew' – those knowing the Law but

being deficient in some way from full participation in the worship of the Temple.

6. We have, of course, to be cautious in using the speeches in Acts. Even on a straightforward reading it is clear that much has been omitted, e.g. there is no introduction to the person of Jesus: he is simply spoken of as the Resurrected One. Nevertheless the difference between the Athens sermon and the rest of Acts cannot be fortuitous: the author was trying to tell us of the different style which Paul employed in addressing a purely Gentile audience.

7. I am not saying that these campaigners are right – the interesting thing is the extreme reaction against them.

8. *The Gospel in a Pluralist Culture* (1989). Cf. also the publication of the Church of England Board of Mission *The Gospel in our Time*.

9. Sadly, through a misreading of Genesis 1 and 2, and because of the apparent marginalisation of the feminine, many involved in the Green Movement are antipathetic to the Judaeo-Christian tradition. There is a great need to show them the gospel which the Bible has for just this situation.

10. Though even in a more homogeneous social setting at the turn of the century this was not always true in fact – the carriage trade came in the morning and the servants in the evening.

11. First printed in *The Church of England Newspaper*.

12. Cf. *All God's Children?* (1991).

13. Research has shown that 60 per cent of people prayed regularly – i.e. not just in crisis situations. Put alongside other findings that only 34 per cent of people believe in a personal God it makes one wonder who or what they were praying to. But as an example of the continuation of religious belief and practice it is impressive. It can well be used in evangelism – 'the unknown God' – 'what you worship but do not know – this is what I now proclaim' (Acts 17:23).

14. I remember my own sense of shock in 1975 when a well-educated woman came and said, 'What are these Gospels you have been talking about?' and, when I showed her Matthew, Mark, Luke and John said, 'That looks interesting; I have heard of the Bible but never seen one.' Her next comment was, 'What are all the numbers down the side?' – she had never used chapter and verse. Such lack of knowledge was noticeable in the mid–70s. It would be less remarkable now.

Chapter 3. Joining the Kingdom

1. This diagram is almost entirely the work of Felicity Lawson, Director of Ministerial Training in the Diocese of Wakefield, and can be found in *Saints Alive!* published by Anglican Renewal Ministries. I am most grateful for permission to reproduce it: the comments are all my own.
2. Cf. John 3:8; Ezek. 37:9f.
3. Often it is found that those who have spoken in tongues have only done so once or twice – they have never been encouraged to use it regularly as a prayer language.
4. Needless to say, there is also a down-side – churches divided and individuals hurt. But overall there can be little doubt that the Charismatic Movement has been of the greatest importance in the life of the Church.

Chapter 4. Strategy for Evangelism – I

1. The term 'church committee' is used throughout the book to denote the decision-making body in the church. Different denominations call it different things – it may be the Stewards' Meeting, the Parochial Church Council, the Church Meeting, etc., etc.
2. From the meeting of the Anglican primates at Larnaca, 1989.
3. *Evangelisation in the Modern World* (1974). The use by Roman Catholics and others (including many Pentecostals) of the word evangelisation deserves explanation. It is often seen as representing a more holistic view of God's mission in the world which comprises the conversion of society and the cosmos as well as individuals. In this perspective 'evangelism' is seen as narrowly confined to the conversion of individuals. However, it is doubtful if this can be maintained for much longer. Evangelism is now seen in wider terms than simply seeking 'the salvation of souls' by most except the more old-fashioned Evangelicals, and there is a realisation that changed lives are essential to holistic evangelisation. I find that the terms are often used interchangeably by both Roman Catholics and others, though some wish to retain a distinction. In everyday use the answer is to use the verb 'evangelise', which has the benefit that it suggests action!
4. Matthew 28:19.
5. The debate which seeks to polarise these first two elements of evangelism – i.e. the individual and corporate aspects of the

gospel – now seems to be largely resolved. The Lausanne statement from the Evangelicals and the acceptance of the need for
personal 'metanoia' by those who would previously have held a
'social gospel' is taking much of the acrimony from this debate.

6. 1 Thessalonians 1:5.

7. *The Logic of Evangelism* (1989).

8. *The Normal Christian Birth* (1989).

9. In the Theological Appendix to *Saints Alive!* (Anglican Renewal
   Ministries, 3rd edition, 1990).

10. Archbishop Robert Runcie.

11. This phrase is not theologically exact, and may be described in
    other terms – 'renewal in the Spirit', 'the fullness of the Spirit',
    'receiving the Spirit'. The term used is not important, the reality
    is.

12. John 15:16 and all the passages which speak of the grace of God
    who of his own good will 'gave gospel'.

13. These are not all to do with 'conversion': a summary of the
    findings are in *Seeing the Invisible*, Meg Maxwell and Verena
    Tschudin (1990).

14. This Churches Together in England Evangelism Project is
    expected to report in September 1992 and will be followed by
    educational programmes for local churches, theological colleges,
    etc.

15. Further interim figures are given in *Understanding Leadership*
    (Darton, Longman and Todd, 1989).

16. *Dynamics of Spiritual Life* (1989).

17. He ate and drank with 'sinners', made sure that his wedding
    party host did not suffer social embarrassment and provided food
    for the hungry.

18. 'God will provide'.

Chapter 5. Strategy for Evangelism – II

1. John 10:10 – *perissos* has the idea of having more than one needs,
   of overflowing abundance.

2. Every minister has his or her own story of the depths of ignorance
   – a Roman Catholic bishop told me of a visit to a school (RC!)
   where a sixteen-year-old asked him who the 'little man' on his
   pectoral crucifix was. A survey in 1991 showed that a third of
   people did not know what Easter commemorated.

3. In my experience a situation where a 'strict' baptism policy is in
   force often makes evangelism difficult because 'they wouldn't do

our baby'. However, there is an important exception: where the minister appeared friendly, concerned and helpful, the negative feelings were largely dissipated. Resentment occurs when young parents are bewildered by the attitude of a minister who is saying to himself, 'Oh dear, here is another theological conundrum'.

4. Although I would not wish to make it an article of faith I believe that the gift of an evangelist is not one which primarily is to do with words – it is to make an invitation so that others will respond. I have heard so many poor evangelistic addresses by an evangelist which have brought a large response and so many excellent addresses which brought no response that I think it is the effectiveness rather than the words of an evangelist which are important. Billy Graham is a good example – his preaching is very variable, but the response to his very low key 'appeal' is extraordinary.

5. Said by John Wesley whose character mirrored that of Paul in many ways. The words were said in exasperation at those who were trying to confine his ministry within the parochial system of the Church of England.

6. All Church Army Officers are commissioned as evangelists, but the difficulty which they recognise is that not all of them are truly evangelists – besides not all evangelists want to become Church Army officers.

7. Cf. Romans 8:16. 'The Spirit himself testifies with our spirit that we are children of God'. This is spoken of that sense of belonging which is so precious to the Christian but that double testimony of the Holy Spirit and the human spirit should be part of all Christian vocation.

8. 1 John 4:18.

9. 1 Corinthians 2:3.

10. The need for theological students 'to move away from the underlying, often unacknowledged, fear of secular society and culture' was mentioned by the Roman Catholic Bishops' Conference in 1990.

Chapter 6. Leading for Mission

1. A distinction is sometimes made between authority and power, stating that the first is the right to control others while power is what others perceive a person to possess. Authority stresses the legal right to command while power is perceived by those being

commanded. However, there are so many exceptions that the words are used almost interchangeably.

2. An alternative pattern is that given by Etzioni in *Modern Organizations* (1964), who classifies power as coercive, remunerative or normative (giving prestige). People's reaction to these kinds of power is alienative (against their wishes), calculative (receiving external rewards) or moral (where they believe in the goals of the organisation). Each kind of power tends to go with a person's involvement with it: hence in churches normative power is often associated with moral involvement.

3. This chimes in well with the 'acceptance theory' of Bernard and Simon who argued that a communication only carried authority when it is accepted by the receiver.

4. John 20:23.

5. Sometimes called 'the ten o'clock knock'. The process begins with two smartly dressed strangers sitting in church for the Sunday services. If they like what they see and hear they will visit the minister later that evening to offer a better rewarded position.

6. While this is seen at its most servile in semi-feudal settings where the squire insists on certain forms of service etc., it can also occur in churches which see themselves as 'the best club in town': the minister is supposed to be amiable, uncontroversial, pliable.

7. Cf. Michael Maccoby, *The Gamesman: the New Corporate Leaders* (1978). The other styles he distinguishes are the Company Man who submerges his identity in the organisation, the Gamesman who always needs a challenge for his team, and the Craftsman who likes doing his own thing. They are not as far distant from the Christian ministry as they ought to be.

8. The most horrific example of this was in a tract I picked up in the Roman Catholic cathedral in Galway in the 1950s. The worst agonies were reserved for those who married Protestants.

9. Acts 23:1–4.

10. 2 Kings 4:9.

11. In logic the term 'referent' is used for the object which is under discussion, or the first term in a premise.

12. The number of people over whom this personal charisma holds sway is sometimes known as the 'fief'. Max Weber noted that such people often were not noticed by the institution. However, when they were, there followed the 'routinization of charisma' where the fief over a period of time moved to being a bureaucracy as the organisation tried to inject some stability into what it saw as an inherently transient and unstable transactional form.

13. Maggie Ross is the pseudonym of an American nun living in Britain who wrote *Pillars of Flame* (1988).
14. *Beyond Bureaucracy* (1976).

Chapter 7. Managing for Mission

1. Research and Development.
2. 'Friction inevitably seems to occur between line and staff (i.e. knowledge) managers. Neither side may fully understand or appreciate the purpose and role of the other. Staff managers are often criticised for unnecessary interference in the work of the line manager and for being out of touch with practical realities. Line managers may feel that the staff managers have an easier and less demanding job because they have no direct responsibility for producing a product or providing a service to the customer, and are free from day-to-day operational problems . . . a major source of difficulty for staff managers is to persuade line managers to accept, and act upon, the advice and recommendations which are offered', Laurie Mullins, *Management and Organisational Behaviour* (1985).
3. For some reason, outsiders see the ability to take a wedding or a funeral as particularly impressive – while in fact they are comparatively straightforward.
4. P. F. Drucker, *Management* (1977).
5. In previous generations promotion often went with length of service: no longer. Now people feel increasingly deskilled, overtaken by younger men and women whom they themselves trained, and sidelined when new opportunities occur.
6. Billy Graham is an exception to this rule – as to almost every other.
7. This will be an increasingly normal way of working. Allied Dunbar, a financial services firm, has 3000 people working in its offices, but a further 5000 self-employed 'associates' working from home.
8. John 8:7; Luke 5:23.
9. Cf. Colette Dowling, *The Cinderella Complex* (1981).
10. This is also true of those from an Asian background. However, research showed that black women were as ready as black (or white) men to confront their supervisors, cf. *The Cinderella Complex*.
11. Cf. John Mole, *Mind Your Manners* (1990).
12. *New Realities* (1989).

13. Peter Drucker is himself a good example of this. *New Realities* was published when he was 80 and he still keeps up a punishing routine of lecturing and writing.

Chapter 8. *Clearing the Undergrowth*

1. Fred Luthans in *Real Managers* (1988) found that managers who spent most time socialising and politiking got promoted but were not the most effective in getting the job done.
2. Many have said that they identify with one of my inefficiencies: if I have two important letters to answer, I pick up the first, read it and put it down. Then I pick up the second, read it, put it down – and then go and have a cup of coffee. In animal studies it is called 'displacement behaviour'.
3. Laurie Mullins, *Management and Organisational Behaviour* (1985). He distinguishes efficiency which is 'doing things right' from effectiveness – 'doing the right things'.
4. *The New Wine* (1986).
5. Ronald Knox in *Enthusiasm* said, 'Men will not live without vision . . . if we are content with the humdrum, the second-best, that hand-over-hand, it will not be forgiven us.'
6. 'The more unpleasant it is, the more urgent it is'. This dictum from J. D. Stewart of Lincoln College in New Zealand reflects our normal unwillingness to tackle the difficult things first.
7. Rosemary Stewart, *Managers and Their Jobs* (1967).
8. Though note that these meetings are not primarily for personal support (unless that is one of the agreed reasons for having the meetings). I have found too many of such gatherings waste time dealing with the personal problems of the leaders rather than seeking God's will for the church.
9. Editorial in *Journal of the Royal College of General Practitioners* (1989).
10. Kirk, *Beauty and Bands*. Perhaps Soapy Sam's joy in administration reminds us that in the church we use the word administration in a pastoral sense, in such phrases as 'the administration of Holy Communion'.
11. This was movingly put by T. W. Manson, 'In the Kingdom of God service is not a stepping stone to nobility: it is nobility, the only kind that is recognised.' However fine the words, it is a useful corrective to remember that there are far more references to the Christian leader as a servant of God than as a servant of others.

12. Of the Manchester University Institute of Science and Technology.
13. Cited by Dr Andrew Melhuish, medical adviser to the Henley Management College.
14. This is closely linked with the need for 'terms of office': cf. *Understanding Leadership*, p. 82.

Chapter 9. Moving into Mission

1. This section deals with the personal accountability of a Christian leader. It does not deal with the corporate accountability of a church or a grouping which is seen in mission audit and such procedures. For these, see my book *The Well Church Book* (1991).
2. Cf. D. McGregor in *An Uneasy Look at Peformance Appraisal* (1957).
3. This does not necessarily have to be at the end of the time. Often I have found that midway through the interview enables profound things to surface. It can be like taking a step into a more real and deeper place.
4. The basic ideas can be found in *The Unblocked Manager* by Mike Woodcock and Dave Francis (1982).
5. Management theory tends to think primarily of line management and therefore deals most with those above and below in a hierarchical structure. However, sideways relationships which are built upon friendship and common interest rather than authority are often far more influential.
6. The popularity and effectiveness of the Ignatian retreat comes from a considerable stretch of time being deliberately given to God.
7. Gallwey, *The Inner Game of Tennis* (1974).
8. Philip Greenslade, *Leadership* (1984).
9. The disciple John.
10. Judson Cornwall, *Profiles of a Leader* (1980).

Chapter 10. The Spirituality of Evangelism

1. Widespread interest in psychological manipulation goes back to the Korean war and the effect of 'brainwashing' on prisoners of war.
2. An excellent review of the tele-evangelists is given by the

sociologist Steve Bruce in *Pray TV* (1990). He says the effect of these evangelists has been much exaggerated, since they spoke mainly to the converted. It may be that the disgrace of Jimmy Swaggert and the others has meant that this type of evangelism is being re-evaluated and more wholesome patterns are emerging.

3. Just as 1 Corinthians 13:1–3 describes the essential nature of love so 1 Corinthians 13:4–7 describes the characteristics of love and hence of true evangelism: 'Evangelism is patient and kind. Evangelism envies no one, is never boastful, never conceited, never rude; evangelism is never selfish, never quick to take offence. Evangelism keeps no score of wrongs, takes no pleasure in the sins of others, but delights in the truth. There is nothing evangelism cannot face; there is no limit to its faith, its hope, its endurance.'

4. In *The Cross and the Switchblade* (1965).

5. One minister mentioned that a turning-point in his ministry came when he realised that because he had not wept with the mourners he had been unable to 'rejoice with those who rejoice'. He had kept within a narrow band of emotion without extremes. He spoke of the new-found sympathy with people this had led to and how it had had repercussions in other areas of his life, not least his marriage.

6. Samuel Rutherford: seventeenth-century Scottish Covenanter who used his letters to help people towards God.

7. Philippians 4:1. Cf. also 1 Thessalonians 2:19f, 2 Timothy 1:4.

8. 2 Timothy 1:6.

9. From an address at the Anglican Evangelical Assembly in 1991.

10. 'I don't know what you mean by "glory",' said Alice . . .
'I meant "there's a nice knock-down argument for you!" '
'But "glory" doesn't mean "a nice knock-down argument," ' Alice objected.
'When *I* use a word,' Humpty Dumpty said, in a rather scornful tone, 'it means just what I choose it to mean – neither more nor less.' *Through the Looking Glass*, Lewis Carroll.

Bibliography

These books deal primarily with those areas of mission covered in this book. A bibliography covering Christian leadership can be found in my previous book *Understanding Leadership* (DLT 1989).

Theology

Abraham, W., *The Logic of Evangelism* (Hodder, 1989).
Bosch, D., *Transforming Mission* (Orbis, 1991).
Cotterell, P., *Mission and Meaninglessness* (SPCK, 1990).
Green, M., *Evangelism in the Early Church* (Highland, 1984).
Marshall, M., *The Gospel Connection* (DLT, 1990).
McDonnell, K. and Montague, G., *Christian Initiation and Baptism in the Holy Spirit* (Michael Glazier, 1991).
Papal Encyclical, *Evangelisation in the Modern World* (Catholic Truth Society, 1974).
Reid, G., *Redescribing Evangelism* (BCC, 1989).
Samuel, V. and Hansen, A., *Proclaiming Christ in Christ's Way* (Regnum, 1989).
Stott, J., *Christian Mission in the Modern World* (Falcon, 1975).
Watson, D., *I Believe in Evangelism* (Hodder, 1984).

Gospel and culture

Board of Mission and Unity, *The Gospel in our Time* (BMU).
Donovan, V. J., *Christianity Rediscovered* (SCM, 1978).
Newbigin, L., *The Gospel in a Pluralist Culture* (SPCK, 1989).

Journey into Faith

Hill, M., *Entering the Kingdom* (MARC, 1986).
Pawson, D., *The Normal Christian Birth* (Hodder, 1989).
Toon, P., *About Turn* (Hodder, 1987).
Wallis, J., *The Call to Conversion* (Lion, 1984).

Nurture group/Catechumenate

Additional Curates Society, *Follow Me*.
Ball, P., *Journey into Faith* (SPCK, 1984).
Bible Reading Fellowship, *Thank God for That*.
Bible Society, *Caring for New Christians*.
Church Pastoral Aid Society, *Christian Basics*.
Grundy, M., *Evangelisation Through the Adult Catechumenate* (Grove Books, 1991).
Lawson, F. and Finney, J., *Saints Alive!* (Anglican Renewal Ministries).

Mission Audit

Board of Mission, *An Audit for the Local Church*.
Diocese of Southwell, *Forward in Faith*. (Obtainable from 39 Davies Road, West Bridgford, Nottingham NG2 5JE.)
Finney, J., *The Well Church Book* (CPAS/SU, 1991).
URC Supplies, *Mission Pursuit*. (Obtainable from 86 Tavistock Place, London WC1 9RT.)